# Educational Research
# and Evaluation

# Educational Research and Evaluation:
## For Policy and Practice?

*Edited by*

## Robert G. Burgess

 The Falmer Press

(A member of the Taylor & Francis Group)
London • Washington, DC

| | |
|---|---|
| UK | The Falmer Press, 4 John St, London WC1N 2ET |
| USA | The Falmer Press, Taylor & Francis Inc., 1900 Frost Road, Suite 101, Bristol, PA 19007 |

---

First published 1993

**A catalogue record of this publication is available from the British Library**

ISBN 0 75070 188 9 cased
ISBN 0 75070 189 7 paperback

**Library of Congress Cataloging-in-Publication Data are available on request**

Jacket design by Caroline Archer

Typeset in 11/13pt Bembo by
Graphicraft Typesetters Ltd., Hong Kong

*Printed in Great Britain by Burgess Science Press, Basingstoke on paper which has a specified pH value on final paper manufacture of not less than 7.5 and is therefore 'acid free'.*

# Contents

Contents

# List of Abbreviations

APU          Assessment of Performance Unit
BERA        British Educational Research Association
CARE        Centre for Applied Research in Education
CBI          Confederation of British Industry
CEDAR     Centre for Educational Development, Appraisal and Research
DES          Department of Education and Science
DoH         Department of Health
DSS         Department of Social Security
DTI          Department of Trade and Industry
EHE         Enterprise in Higher Education
EPA         Educational Priority Area
ESG         Education Support Grant
ESRC        Economic and Social Research Council
FE           Further Education
FEU         Further Education Unit
GAO        General Accounting Office
GCSE       General Certificate of Secondary Education
GRIDS      Guidelines of Review and Internal Development of Schools
GRIST      Grant Related In-Service Training
HEI          Higher Education Institution
HMI         Her Majesty's Inspectorate
HMSO      Her Majesty's Stationery Office
ILEA        Inner London Education Authority
IMET       Inspection Methodologies for Education and Training
INSET      In-Service Education and Training
LAPP       Lower Achieving Pupils Project
LEA         Local Education Authority

| | |
|---|---|
| LEATGS | Local Education Authority Training Grants Schemes |
| LMS | Local Management of Schools |
| MSC | Manpower Services Commission |
| NAEP | National Assessment of Educational Progress |
| NFER | National Foundation for Educational Research |
| PEMD | Program Evaluation and Methodology Division |
| PRAISE | Pilot Records of Achievement in Schools Evaluation |
| R & D | Research and Development |
| RANSC | Records of Achievement National Steering Committee |
| RESC | Records of Achievement Extension Steering Committee |
| SAT | Standard Assessment Test |
| SCI | Senior Chief Inspector |
| SEAC | School Examinations and Assessment Council |
| SSE | School Self-Evaluation |
| TA | Training Agency |
| TC | Training Commission |
| TGAT | Task Group on Assessment and Testing |
| TVEE | Technical and Vocational Ecucation Extension |
| TVEI | Technical and Vocational Education Initiative |

# Preface

Although much has been written on styles, strategies and tactics associated with educational research and evaluation, there is still relatively little on the social processes associated with the methodology. Furthermore, there are very few books that explicitly consider the relationship of research and evaluation to policy and practice. On this basis, a conference which was held at the Centre for Educational Development, Appraisal and Research (CEDAR) at the University of Warwick focused on this issue through a series of papers that were intended to address policy-makers and practitioners as well as academics and researchers. The papers at the conference were generally very well received and have therefore been produced as a collection that is intended to appeal to a wide audience in Britain and the USA, and in other parts of the English-speaking world.

The material is a resource for students, researchers, academics, policy-makers and practitioners. It is intended to open up key debates in the field of educational research and evaluation; identify some of the key processes involved; examine the problems of conducting research and evaluation and the ways in which they can be overcome; and provide actual examples of the processes and problems as they occur in a range of projects.

The volume begins with an essay that outlines some of the major issues and problems involved in the conduct of studies directed towards educational policy and practice. In Part One, the papers are concerned with the relationship between the contractor and the customer (Burgess), research and evaluation for local education authorities (Sanday), studies for government (in this case, the United States) (Chelimsky and Mulhauser), the representation of the voices of the researched in an evaluation for policy-makers (Biott) and inspection as a form of evaluation (Wilcox).

In Part Two all the papers are based on empirical examples of conducting educational research and evaluation. Some of the issues involved are: local and national evaluations in education (Pole), the evaluation of records of achievement (James), the study of primary schooling (Nias) and the use of research in professional development (Holly).

All together these chapters examine a range of different dimensions associated with educational research and evaluation that is conducted for policy and practice.

In preparing these papers for publication special credit should be given to Malcolm Clarkson and the Falmer Press that sponsored the original conference. In addition, my thanks are due to all the CEDAR staff and secretaries (especially Janet Flynn, Pat Lea and Su Powell) for their assistance and support. As with all such volumes, any errors or omissions remain my own.

**Robert G. Burgess**
*University of Warwick*

# 1 Biting the Hand that Feeds You? Educational Research for Policy and Practice

*Robert G. Burgess*

The late 1980s witnessed changes to the styles of social and educational research. In recent years we have seen a shift away from the kind of curriculum research advocated by Michael F.D. Young in the early 1970s when he argued that there was no alternative to researchers devising their own problems on the school curriculum rather than taking questions devised by those actively engaged in policy formulation and the practice of education (Young, 1971). Indeed, in the world of research bids, evaluation studies, contracts and tenders, it is common to find the research problem and the research approach being specified by the sponsor. What, we might ask, are the implications of this move for research? Does it mean that research will no longer or can no longer be independent and critical? Does it mean that researchers are little more than contract labourers whose work is reduced to little more than the application of mere techniques? Does it mean that research in education must become policy-relevant? Does it mean that research must come closer to the requirements of practitioners? In this respect, it is the purpose of this chapter (and of the others in this volume) to examine some of the critical issues associated with research and evaluation in education by focusing on different aspects of the research process. In part, this chapter will be autobiographical as it will draw on my experience as a research director who in the course of negotiating contracts and designing research projects must consider not only how to get funding but also the implications this may hold for the collection, analysis and dissemination of data. In these terms, an analysis of research sponsorship becomes critical, as discussed in the following section.

## Research Sponsorship

Given that research funding is critical to the research process, we might expect that those who have written on research methodology (myself included) might have had something to say about issues raised by research sponsorship. Yet a brief glance at the numerous texts and readers available quickly shows a glaring omission.

My own thoughts on this matter were stimulated by a discussion with a potential sponsor some years ago. The potential sponsor was the education officer of a large private company who had funded educational research and development work in the UK and who expressed interest in some of the work in which I was involved and in funding a conference. On hearing that the conference was concerned with curriculum and assessment policy he had a question to ask: would any of the people giving papers be making political statements or criticizing government policy? My response was to argue that political statements were not part of the business of social and educational research but a careful and critical analysis of policy and practice was part of the research agenda. At this point, the potential sponsor indicated that the directors of his company would not be happy to find that money had been used to voice criticism of government policy. In short, I would need to think if any of my speakers would be criticizing government policy if I was to bid for money from his company. Needless to say that company did not sponsor the conference, nor were they asked. Yet this was not a purely negative experience for it set me thinking about research sponsorship, styles of sponsorship, the involvement of sponsors with researchers and the researched and with activities concerned with development and dissemination.

We should begin by asking: who are the sponsors of educational research and educational evaluation? Here, there are the obvious organizations such as government departments (the Department for Education) and local authorities as well as a range of other government departments: the DSS, the DoH, the DTI and so on, and a number of public and private companies as well as local and national trusts. We might ask, however, what are the terms in which these organizations request research and evaluation bids, issue tender documents and draw up research and evaluation contracts? What are the implications for research, researchers and those who are researched? It is, therefore, appropriate to address these issues through an analysis of the research process.

### *What Kind of Research is Commissioned?*

Anyone who is interested in gaining research funding needs to take account of the specific projects that will be funded by organizations, trusts and government departments. For example, the Department of Education and Science (now the Department for Education) specify that they are concerned to commission or fund projects that are 'policy related' if they:

1 will help to guide policy decisions that need to be taken;
2 will help to improve the quality of the educational process in areas of policy concern;
3 will facilitate the implementation of policy decisions; or
4 will evaluate the effects of the implementation of policy decisions (DES, 1982).

Such a range of projects suggests research, research and development, and evaluation activities. Furthermore, many projects originate within the Department so that they reflect current interests. For example, the Department regularly requests proposals for research-based evaluation of education support grants and, more recently, on curriculum and assessment given the direction of national policy. Similar trends can also be seen in requests to tender for research from such diverse organizations as the former Training Agency and the Economic and Social Research Council (ESRC) where initiatives such as Information Technology and Education result in a careful specification of project areas and project evaluation that is supported by research council money.

At this stage, researchers need to consider areas in which they have substantive and methodological competence to get involved. However, it does not end there. In some cases, budgets are small, time-scales short and a field force is assumed to be on stand-by to conduct fieldwork should the research bid be successful. Here consideration needs to be given to a number of issues by the researcher and by the research sponsor:

1 Are the funds that are available sufficient to hire adequately trained staff with the appropriate training, research skills and substantive experience?

2   Are the time-scales appropriate? Often tender documents spe-
    cify a time budget (which is important if the project staff are
    to meet deadlines). However, it is important to consider
    whether sufficient time has been given to data collection and
    analysis, especially where case-study methods are specified. For
    example, some organizations consider that case-studies can be
    conducted in five days. In these circumstances, the research
    community needs to discuss carefully with the sponsor the
    expectations in terms of methodology.

3   Can appropriate staff be recruited in time for the project? Un-
    less core funds are provided for a research centre or a depart-
    ment, it is virtually impossible to have a field force on stand-by
    in the way that market research companies have interviewers
    available. Furthermore, once we move beyond the 'standard
    interview' to engage in observational work and the analysis of
    documents, a broader range of skills are required.

More fundamental than these questions, however, is the topic to be
researched.

### What Is to Be Researched?

We have already acknowledged that there has been a change from
problems specified by the researcher to a situation where research
issues are specified by the sponsor. Here, we should recall the advice
given by Lawrence Stenhouse (1984) on relations between proposal
writing and sponsorship:

> When it comes to research aims, I think I have always worked
> with double sets of aims — one for the sponsor and one for
> myself! The proposal sets out the job I hope to do for the
> sponsor. . . . The whole art of funded research is to find scope
> for your own aims within and alongside the sponsor's aims —
> and without costing the sponsor anything (p. 213).

How might this duality work in practice? Here, I turn to a request I
received from the Assessment of Performance Unit to tender for a
four-year programme of work that involved a survey of 7-year-old
pupils. The tender briefing documents stated that proposals will:

1   develop a variety of test instruments within and across the core
    curriculum of English language, mathematics, science and

technology (as in the proposed National Curriculum) for 7-year-old pupils;

2 conduct a national survey in 1991 of the performance in the core curriculum areas of top infant pupils of all abilities, drawn from maintained and independent schools in England, Wales and Northern Ireland;

3 analyze the resulting data and produce a report thereon;

4 prepare appropriate materials for disseminating the findings from the survey so as to assist teachers in assessing children of this age group as well as enabling them to appreciate the relevance of the findings to their teaching practices (APU, 1988).

Such a programme of work raised several issues that had to be addressed prior to writing the proposal. First, is this the kind of work in which one wished to be involved? Second, did our team have the necessary expertise for such a project? Finally, could we manage such a project and keep to deadlines? In answer to these questions, first, the project aims signalled that research and development activities were to be involved in close liaison with schools, pupils and teachers. In these circumstances, it appeared that we would be able to engage in research-based development activity in the field of curriculum and assessment. Second, we did have expertise in research on curriculum and assessment, and in the methodology that was required. Furthermore, we did have links with a variety of local authorities, schools and teachers throughout the country which would facilitate such work. Finally, our experience involved working to deadlines — an essential requirement in this project as anyone who took on the project and failed to meet the deadline of having all test instruments prepared for the 1991 survey would be in considerable difficulty. On this basis, it seemed we were an appropriate organization to mount a bid given the degree of close correspondence between our aims and those of the potential sponsor.

Yet in any proposal it becomes important to work within and go beyond the aims and objectives that have been carefully specified by the sponsor. Furthermore, it is essential to demonstrate the key elements of the project that would be examined. In our proposal I specified six issues that emerged from the tender document and which would link with our interests and expertise. They were:

1 the importance of focusing on the curriculum in English language, mathematics, science and technology together with the implications for assessment and testing;

2 the importance of cross-curricular and subject-integrated approaches which are consistent with the attainment targets drawn up by the Mathematics and Science Working Groups;
3 the relationship of continuous assessment and standardized assessment tasks to the programmes of study drawn up by the Working Groups;
4 the importance of development and trialling of test items;
5 the moderation of tests by teachers;
6 systematic training in assessment procedures for teachers.

Here, I saw the importance attached not only in the briefing document but also in the TGAT report (DES, 1987a) to links made between the curriculum, assessment and testing so much so that detailed first-hand observations would need to be made of current curriculum content and current procedures for assessment and testing in a range of infant schools. In short, it was an opportunity within the project aims to document variations in the pattern of 'delivery' of the National Curriculum as we had yet to discover how infant school teachers in state and independent schools in different areas of England and Wales would come to terms with teaching a range of subjects to infant pupils. Second, it provided an opportunity to make comparisons across the state and independent sectors not only of curriculum delivery but also of performance and the way in which testing and assessment took place in different social settings. Third, it allowed case-studies and multi-site case-studies (thirty-two in my proposal) to be used for pilot work and data collection as a basis for the development and trialling of test items prior to the National Survey in 1991. The conceptual framework of the project therefore involved the construction of tests from aspects of practice which were compatible with the National Curriculum but were not directly specified in it; we had to keep in mind a principle that Stenhouse identified in his classic text *An Introduction to Curriculum Research and Development* where he stated:

> For a curriculum one does not look at a book but at the school. If curriculum is defined in this way, then the study of curriculum can be reduced to the empirical study of schools. The curriculum is not the intention or prescription but what happens in real situations. It is not the aspiration, but the achievement. The problem of specifying the curriculum is one of perceiving, understanding and describing what is actually going on in school and classroom (1975, p. 2).

On this basis, he argued that we need to examine the school as an agency of teaching and learning, based on the interpretation of careful observation.

Certainly, it was this approach that appeared in our proposal where we developed the case-study approach to a multi-site case-study which facilitated making comparisons on curriculum and assessment but where, as an additional spin-off, further work could be done on the use of the case-study and multi-site case-study in research and development activities on curriculum and assessment as thirty-two schools would be used for the following purposes:

1   To conduct observational studies in schools and classrooms so as to identify some of the key features of English, mathematics, science and technology and strategies for testing in these areas. Here, the researchers would need to work alongside advisers, teachers and pupils. These observations would be complemented by in-depth interviews with advisers and teachers about:

      i   curriculum content,
     ii   skills training, and
    iii   testing procedures.

    In addition, the observational and interview material would need to be complemented with documentary evidence obtained from the schools in the form of syllabuses, schemes of work, tests and assessment schemes. This work would be conducted simultaneously with test development. It would therefore allow the project team to see how infant teachers were simultaneously handling the National Curriculum and test procedures.
2   To evaluate the ways in which teachers use the tests, the process of moderation and the ways in which 'results' are utilized with pupils, parents and other teachers.
3   To examine the technical and social problems involved in reporting on the performance of whole classes and whole schools.

On this basis the data collection and analysis was intended to explore some of the problematic issues associated with assessment and testing prior to the National Survey in 1991.

It was the basis of this pilot work that our team would develop:

1   Test and assessment items involving:

 i  Traditional pencil and paper tests,
 ii computer-based tests,
 iii oral presentations,
 iv observational work by teachers, and
 v group tests.

Here, it would be essential to look at issues of reliability and validity within and between the test items. Validation will involve norm-referenced as well as criterion-referenced test instruments.

2   Test and assessment items that involve:

 i a particular subject area, and
 ii cross-curricular work.

Here, test administration involves: the collection of systematic data based on pupil performance, the training of teachers in test administration and moderation and the training of teachers in using assessment as a basis of improved practice with individual children and whole classes. Such a range of issues that facilitate research and research-based development activities fit well with our aims and, we hope, the sponsor's.

Research does not merely rely on the substantive issues, such as curriculum, assessment, testing, records of achievement or whatever, but also on principles of method. It is therefore to a consideration of some methodological principles that we now turn.

### Research Design

In some projects, the sponsor may be more concerned with matters of substance than the way the research is to be conducted. In other cases, however, there is a careful specification of the way in which the work is to be conducted.

One example comes from a project that was successfully bid for which involved evaluation of an activity that had been supported by an Education Support Grant (ESG). Here, local authorities were required to bid for money to support the activity but in their letter of award they were reminded:

The letter to LEAs setting out successful bids makes it clear that the Secretary of State attaches particular importance to monitoring and evaluation by LEAs of ESG projects and wishes to ensure that each project has indentifiable objectives which are capable of measurement of achievement at each stage. You will recall that the Draft Education Support Grants Circular issued on 30 July 1987 stated that LEAs would be required to evaluate records of achievement work against criteria and outcomes to be specified by the Secretary of State. With this in mind I would ask that your LEA begin preparing proposals for the evaluation of your project's work, with a view to submitting these to the Department . . . (DES, 1987b).

At first glance, it appears that the emphasis is upon a quantitative evaluation, as we are told that each project must have '. . . objectives which are capable of measurement at each stage'. Yet on turning the page we find that authorities were told that:

In drawing up proposals I would ask your LEA to bear in mind the following criteria. The evaluation should:

— address both the issues you have been asked to investigate, as identified above;
— be carried out by a person (or persons) who is independent of the project team, and who has proven experience of evaluation (or for whom adequate professional supervision can be guaranteed);
— be conducted in such a manner that the national evaluators could cross-validate the findings;
— generate evidence that others would have access to (under appropriate ethical safeguards), in the form of a case record (DES, 1987b).

Here, the ground rules have changed as the language associated with quantitative work has suddenly been replaced by words that suggest a qualitative evaluation. Furthermore, a very specific form of qualitative-based investigation is suggested, including a case-record approach — a term devised by Lawrence Stenhouse to refer to material such as fieldnotes, documents, and interview transcripts that could be kept in an archive and used as a basis for producing case-studies. Furthermore, he advocated that case-records could be used by other researchers to examine issues common to a variety of research sites. It was therefore not unusual to find that members of the local authority who received this letter were not only unclear about what constituted a case-record but also the cost involved in conducting such work. I was requested to write the proposal for the research-based evaluation and also to do the work. However, in working within a set of principles of research design it becomes important:

1  to establish clear links between the problem and the appropriate methods of investigation;
2  to specify the staff (research and secretarial) that would be required for the specified activities;
3  to indicate the costs that are involved in the production of case-records and case-studies in this instance.

All these are important issues to resolve at the time of proposal writing so that the processes and products can be specified and agreed by both the sponsor and the researcher, as many misunderstandings at the reporting stage can be avoided. In particular, consideration needs to be given to the procedures to be adopted in collecting, analyzing and disseminating data.

## Collecting and Analyzing Data

In all research and evaluation the method of investigation must be appropriate for the problem at hand. In this sense, we cannot automatically determine that qualitative methods or case-study investigation will be used in any study. Furthermore, we need to think of the ways in which quantitative and qualitative data may be used in research (Bryman, 1988). However, it is also necessary to specify what we mean by certain methods.

Earlier in the chapter I have indicated the ways in which I see case-study methods being used to get access to the day-to-day activities associated with the teaching, learning and assessment process, but what do we mean by the term 'case-study'? Here, I take case-study methods to include observation, participant observation, unstructured interviews, group interviews and discussions and written, oral and visual evidence that is derived from documents. However, there is no 'standard' way in which these methods can be used. Studies based on observation and participant observation have traditionally involved periods of a year or more where researchers have conducted fieldwork to produce ethnographic studies of schools and classrooms (for example, Ball, 1981;

Burgess, 1983). In addition, case-study methods have also involved 'condensed fieldwork' where the researcher may only spend up to twelve to fifteen days in a school and where unstructured interviews and conversations complemented by a small amount of observation become the main method of investigation (Walker, 1974; Stenhouse, 1982, 1984).

In turn, potential sponsors may have other ideas about case-study. For example, within many organizations much interest is shown in case-study but it is apparent that this has to keep up with the momentum of the situations studied. A request to study twelve locations in the UK over a period of a month, where courses were being delivered over twenty days, presented a problem. First, how can the researcher utilize case study methods? Second, how can these methods be used to get access to the depth and detail associated with the way in which individuals live their lives? Here, issues of sampling and selection are involved together with time budgets and the availability of staff. In such circumstances, given the location of the twelve sites throughout the UK, four sites might be selected to provide contrast in terms of geography as well as institutional status. Second, a range of methods may be used. Some observation of the settings, together with documentary materials on the courses in question may be used to construct unstructured interview agendas. However, a further advantage to case-study methods is that participants may be encouraged to record their own observations first-hand by keeping diaries throughout the period of the course. In short, different methods can be used to generate valid and reliable data that have been obtained using different approaches.

However, methodology may have a different emphasis in some projects. One example comes from the tender document produced by the former Training Commission (TC) in requests to bid for the Enterprise in Higher Education (EHE) project which we were told involved a research specification based on case-study methodology for the institutions involved in Enterprise in Higher Education in 1988–89. The details provided in a section headed 'case-study methodology' stated:

8   In 1988–9 up to 11 institutions will be running full EHE projects. Others will be running developmental programmes. It is important at this formative stage for the TC to monitor the development of the initiative as a whole and to identify the processes and relative success of defferent projects. The TC therefore requires an in-depth qualitative study that will provide detailed feedback on the operation and outputs on the EHE projects. Case-studies of the EHE projects in the

fully participant higher education institutions (up to 11) would satisfy this requirement, allowing the collection of data on both processes underlying the working of EHE and the awareness, aptitudes and skills of participants. Thus a study is required that gives information about EHE in each case, a cross-institution picture of EHE, and a thematic analysis of the initiative as a whole in its first year.

9  Classically, comparator groups are used to determine the net effects of policy interventions, although it is recognized that there are particular difficulties in establishing a comparator group of non-EHE students and staff in this research. Potential contractors are asked to consider possible approaches to establishing a comparator group. For instance two of the institutions carrying out developmental work for EHE in 1988–9 might provide a 'comparison group' for comparison with the fully participant institutions. Comparison groups on non-EHE students within HEIs would also be desirable, as appropriate (Training Commission, 1988).

In this instance the language of the project, which in paragraph eight referred to 'in-depth qualitative study' providing 'detailed feedback' on the participants' views of enterprise education, seemed to fit well with qualitative-based case-study research. However, paragraph nine, which discussed comparator groups, seemed to come closer to classic experimental design, while further paragraphs outlined the design of questionnaires to be used in face-to-face interviews together with: 'The use of other approaches to supplement these interviews . . . particularly in the assessment of attitude changes, skills development and the use of new learning methods' (Training Commission, 1988).

In short, the methodology that is called 'case-study' appeared to be shorthand for the detailed study of eleven institutions (in this instance), for the bulk of the methodology appeared to be based on samples and questionnaires more associated with a survey. Here, it was essential to clarify the meaning of different terms and to signal the potential of different methods to deliver the data that were required. Certainly, as Walker (1988) has indicated, it becomes important to modify qualitative methods for use in research that is designed to examine issues relating to policy and practice.

How, we might ask, can this research be applied to practice? Here we consider questions of data analysis and dissemination. First, how might the data be collected and analyzed? Second, how might it be used? As far as data collection is concerned, suitably anonymized material such as interview transcripts may be made publicly available (in what Stenhouse has called the case-record). It is this material that might be used by practitioners to examine their own practice. Here, the analytic categories that are used are not those of the social scientist or educational researcher, but participants' concepts. I have used this approach when asking teachers to keep diaries about their activities in classes where adults rather than pupils are present (Burgess, 1988). In this work, I have used diary entries to build interviews and conversations about initial encounters between teachers and adult students, such as in the following extract where I am talking with an English teacher:

RB: One of the things that I was specifically inter-ested . . . well *the* thing I was specifically interested in here, was the notion of teachers talking about adults in classes and one of the things that you wrote on the first page of this account was to say 'I don't think that all adults are suited to joining infill classes but Susan seems to have fitted in well' — can you say something about why you don't think adults are suited to joining infill classes?

Teacher: Yes. Pupils are used to the exam build, they're trained to some extent in the exam technique, they've just taken their O levels and a lot of adults come to education obviously either never having had any formal education or being in a school is strange to them and it's not to the boys and girls who come into the sixth form and I think you've got to be a pretty strong character to cope with being with some cocky sixth-formers which is what they are. Susan's been lucky because the girls in her group have been sympathetic towards her, they've been helpful when she's missed time, they've given her notes, but that's because she's behaved liked a schoolgirl.

RB: Yes, I've noticed that you've said this in as far that you say 'she fits in with the others' . . . on page 3 of your diary you say 'she fits in with the others by being like them, like a schoolgirl'. Can you explain that? Can you explain how she handles herself in terms of that? Can you describe the attributes that she takes on?

Teacher: It's just a feeling I have. She'll discuss things on the same level as them. When, particularly in a literature class you get on to talk about other things besides the text or things that come out of the text, she will discuss things with them as they discuss them.

RB: So does that . . .

Teacher: Whereas she's obviously actually got a lot more experience . . .

RB: Mmm.

Teacher: Which is good. She brings her experience to lessons but she's obviously got a much more painful experience to bring as well, talking of Susan's case, which presumably is of her own, that she's not talking about, you know, because she's arrived, she's a mother and she's all these other things that they haven't got and she draws on a lot of the things and actually in a way talks too openly, too schoolgirlish, but there's another area that's . . . does it make sense? All her other areas are completely untapped, whereas if I'd got all adults in that class, or all people like Susan — 'cos the thing is again, in an adult class Susan would be different and she may be actually, she might be more closed. I can think of a lot of adult types that would be.

RB: Yes.

Teacher: An adult group she would be less open with but because of what I'm like and what the girls are like, you know, it's the exclusive nature of that group.

Such material may be used in a variety of ways. First, it can be used as a diagnostic tool for individual teachers. Second, such material might be used alongside material collected from other teachers in the same school to consider issues such as adults in classes, adult student and teacher relationships and adult student and pupil relationships. Third, the approach of diary linked to interview is a case-study technique that might be shared with a variety of teachers who might become involved in the process of researching and evaluating their own classroom practice in relation to each other so as to build a series of accounts of classroom practice in their own school (Burgess, 1988). Here, the audience is fellow teachers but what kinds of audiences do we want for research and evaluation based on curriculum and assessment issues?

## Data Dissemination

Issues of dissemination may come at the end of a research project but also need to be considered at the beginning. For those researchers who are sponsored by government departments or by local authorities this issue may arise at the point when a research contract arrives for signature. A contract that has been issued by a government department has caused some concern among researchers, as it states:

12.2 Any publication of research material or of the results of research (as described in sub-paragraph 1 above) or of matters arising from such material or results is subject to the prior consent of the Secretary of State, which consent shall not be unreasonably withheld. Such consent may be given either unconditionally or subject to conditions, in which case any publication shall be subject thereto.

12.3 Where a consent to publication is sought from the Secretary of State, under sub-paragraph 2 above one draft copy of the proposed publication shall be sent to him [sic] at least 28 days before the date intended for submission for publication, so that he may consider not only the content thereof but also may advise the Researcher as to matters pertaining to Crown copyright, royalties and confidentiality. After publication the Researcher shall supply two copies of the publication, free of charge, to the Secretary of State (DHSS, 1987).

Such contracts from the DHSS, the DFE and other government departments raise issues about control of research data relating to their use and publication. Clearly, it is vital for researchers to be able to use their research material in lectures, conference presentations and publications if our knowledge base is to be advanced and if a contribution is to be made to policy and practice. In all cases, researchers need to be aware of issues relating to the law of libel, to confidentiality and to accuracy. Furthermore, when working with schools and teachers, questions about the identifiability of institutions and individuals and the use of pseudonyms must be established at the beginning of a project. Accordingly, in research and development projects in education I would advocate contracts and proposals including a statement on dissemination such as the following:

The dissemination may take a variety of forms:

1 Through papers and discussions to members of the LEA (e.g. groups of advisers, headteachers and teachers);
2 Through a *series* of reports to be delivered to the LEA at *termly* intervals and on other occasions to be agreed, or with a final report at the end of the year;
3 Through the development of an approach that teachers might use to examine school-focused work;
4 Through presentations to professional courses and conferences;
5 Through published work (although agreement needs to be reached on the use of materials) in professional and academic journals.

On this basis there are safeguards for the sponsor and for the researcher. First, the sponsor will obtain direct feedback in a form that is accessible to the participants in the project. Here, such presentations may be oral as well as written. Second, sponsors may get, at the beginning of a project, a commitment to some development work which will assist personnel. Third, researchers may get a commitment that permission to disseminate and to publish will not be withheld, which is essential not only for the advance of knowledge but also for the professional and career development of the researcher concerned who remains in the market-place to make bids and respond to tenders for future projects — a situation where a track record counts.

## Conclusion

In these circumstances we might ask, is there a way forward for the sponsor, the researcher and the teacher engaged in research and development activity? Here, I have suggested issues that all the parties involved in educational research and evaluation might consider relating to the research process. In turn, I have also suggested issues that all the parties need to consider if they are to collaborate successfully. Each of the parties is located in a different context yet each must take account of the social situation and social context of research. Here, researchers might turn back to Stenhouse who remarked:

The crucial problem for curriculum research and study is the development of theory and methodology which is subservient to the needs of teachers and schools. This means that the theory has to be accessible. And it means that the personnel who identify themselves with this field should not allow themselves — or be allowed — to use their knowledge and expertise to divide themselves from teachers. This is an ever-present danger. When it comes to proving oneself as a researcher, the school is often a less attractive setting than the international conference. There is a place for the latter, but not as a substitute for the former (1975, p. 207).

— A timely reminder for social and educational researchers!

## References

ASSESSMENT OF PERFORMANCE UNIT (APU) (1988) *APU: Age 7 Survey* (mimeo).

BALL, S.J. (1981) *Beachside Comprehensive*, Cambridge, Cambridge University Press.

BRYMAN, A. (1988) *Quantitative and Qualitative Social Research*, London, Unwin-Hyman.

BURGESS, R.G. (1983) *Experiencing Comprehensive Education*, London, Methuen.

BURGESS, R.G. (1988) 'Examining classroom practice using diaries and diary interviews, in WOODS, P. and POLLARD, A. (Eds) *Sociology and Teaching: A New Challenge for the Sociology of Education*, London, Croom Helm, pp. 192–208.

DEPARTMENT OF EDUCATION AND SCIENCE (DES) (1982) *Guidance on Application for Financial Support for Educational Research* (mimeo).

DEPARTMENT OF EDUCATION AND SCIENCE (DES) (1987a) *Task Group on Assessment and Testing: A Report*, London, HMSO.

DEPARTMENT OF EDUCATION and SCIENCE (1987b) Personal Correspondence with an LEA Officer.

DEPARTMENT OF HEALTH AND SOCIAL SECURITY (DHSS) (1987) *Standard Conditions for Support for Research Grants made by the Secretary of State for Social Services* (mimeo).

STENHOUSE, L. (1975) *An Introduction to Curriculum Research and Development*, London, Heinemann.

STENHOUSE, L. (1982) 'The conduct, analysis and reporting of case study in educational research and evaluation', in MCCORMICK, R. (Ed.) *Calling Education to Account*, London, Heinemann.

STENHOUSE, L. (1984) 'Library access, library use and user education in academic sixth forms: An autobiographical account', in BURGESS, R.G. (Ed.) *The Research Process in Educational Settings: Ten Case-Studies*, London, Falmer Press, pp. 211–33.

TRAINING COMMISSION (1988) *Research on the Enterprise in Higher Education Initiative: Case-Studies of Institutions Participating in 1988–89* (mimeo).

*Robert G. Burgess*

WALKER, R. (1974) 'The conduct of educational case-study: Ethics, theory and procedures', in MACDONALD, B. and WALKER, R. (Eds) *Innovation, Evaluation, Research and the Problem of Control — Some Interim Papers*, Norwich, CARE, pp. 75–115.

WALKER, R. (1988) 'We would like to know why: Qualitative Research and the Policy-Maker' (mimeo) York, Social Policy Research Unit, University of York.

YOUNG, M.F.D. (1971) 'Introduction', in YOUNG, M.F.D. (Ed.) *Knowledge and Control: New Directions for the Sociology of Education*, New York, Collier-Macmillan.

*Part One*

# Issues in Policy Focused Research and Evaluation

# 2 Contractors and Customers: A Research Relationship?

*Robert G. Burgess*

In the English educational system at present, many relationships have been defined in reports and in legislation. For example, the relationships between local education authorities and schools, between governors and teachers and between teachers and parents have been closely defined. Indeed, within many contemporary initiatives such as the development of records of achievement and the implementation of in-service training, links are suggested between the research community, where local education authorities are required to commission research, and evaluation from independent bodies. Has this particular relationship been defined?

Here we might turn to the HMSO Report of 1971, *The Organization and Management of Government R & D*, a report that drew attention to fundamental distinctions between basic and applied research. Indeed, the report went further by outlining the way in which applied research should be commissioned when it stated:

> This report is based upon the principle that applied R & D, that is R & D with a practical application as its objective, must be done on a contractor–customer basis. The customer says what he [*sic*] wants, the contractor does it (if he can) and the customer pays. Basic, fundamental or pure research . . . has no analogous customer–contractor basis (para. 9).

The main principle of the contractor–customer relationship has now passed into numerous discussions including those concerned with social and educational research. However, we need to ask whether the contractor–customer principle outlined by the Rothschild Report adequately characterizes educational research and evaluation that is commissioned by a government department or a local education authority.

At this point we need to consider the various elements involved in the Rothschild principle and the assumptions involved in it. First, Rothschild draws a distinction between pure and applied research, but can this distinction be made in education? Second, it suggests that the customer knows what is required, that is the kinds of questions that need to be posed, but is this a task that is only for the customer? Has the contractor no role to play? Third, it suggests that the contractor merely carries the work out, a situation that suggests the contractor is a mere technician whose task is to supply 'answers' to the questions that have been posed. This assumption, however, raises the question, is the researcher little more than a technician who provides expertise in order to obtain answers for those engaged in educational policy-making?

Before addressing these questions we need also to remind ourselves that Rothschild excluded social science (including education) from his discussion of applied research. Instead it was included in a further report published in 1982 when he outlined the main purpose of applied social research, which he argued was:

> to provide material on which it may be possible to conduct more informed debate and make better decisions . . . the social science 'customer' includes all those who have a part to play in the decision-making process (para. 3.10).

Clearly, among such customers would be local authorities and government departments and, as Rothschild pointed out, it is important that such research is independent. Nevertheless, he is quick to argue that it is too much to expect decision-making groups to commission research that demonstrates their policies are misconceived, yet he adds, 'but it seems obvious that in many cases the public interest will be served by such research being undertaken' (para. 3.12). In these circumstances, Rothschild has presented the case for applied research informing policy — a situation that appears far removed from the contractor–customer principle. Indeed, it is a situation where a range of research may develop using different strategies.

For those engaged in the educational community as customers and contractors a series of questions should follow about the way in which research is commissioned, designed, conducted, reported and used. Accordingly, I want to address some of these issues drawing on evidence from actual projects in which I have been involved before suggesting a way forward for future research.

## Commissioning Research

The sponsorship of research projects in education is now more likely to come from a government department or a local authority than from a research council or a university. Here we need to consider the kind of research that is being conducted, the reason for which it is being commissioned and the influence this has upon the methodology and the issues that are addressed.

### Issues in Research Design

Many local authorities who are in receipt of funding under the ESG and LEATGS schemes are required to have some kind of independent research and evaluation conducted. However, does it matter if it is research or evaluation? Is there a distinction to be made between the two? Is a compromise made when individuals engage in research-based evaluation? As Janet Finch (1989) has indicated, 'compromise is a key issue', but how do researchers address these issues?

As an example I will discuss a project entitled 'Energy Education and the Curriculum', a short-term project that was commissioned by Hampshire LEA between February and May 1989. This project involved an analysis of the way in which curriculum materials were trialled and used in Hampshire schools. The curriculum materials were based around a series of packs — Sun Monkeys for infant and first school children, Snow Cats for junior and lower secondary pupils and a space project called Tara for secondary children. Our task was specified by the local authority in the following terms:

1 To examine the methods and procedures used on the project with a view to ratifying them;
2 To examine the effectiveness of the teaching materials and teacher use of them;
3 To examine the ease of use of the project materials;
4 To examine the variety of activities involved;
5 To examine the different approaches that schools took when using the project.

Thus the tasks were defined by the team who had designed the project materials. Here, we should note the lack of exploration, enquiry and scepticism attached to our task; we were being asked to verify the procedures used on the project which, it was assumed, were effective, easy to use and resulted in a variety of activities and approaches in Hampshire schools. Here, researchers need to ask whether such a commission is worthy of the term research or evaluation. Indeed, one member of our project team asked: 'Is Hampshire paying us to rubber-stamp their project? Is a seal of good housekeeping all that is required?' Further fundamental issues need to be addressed to make the local authority's questions into researchable topics. Accordingly, in designing a project the tasks defined by Hampshire LEA were taken as a starting point. First, the effectiveness of the teaching materials were questioned. Second, our study set out to find out if there were different ways in which the curriculum project was used by teachers and pupils. Finally, we wished to explore the views of teachers and pupils on the curriculum materials, their links with other aspects of the school curriculum and the National Curriculum. In short, the way in which our project was designed took the local authority agenda as a starting point but added depth and context to the questions that were posed as well as some scepticism (see Shipman, 1988).

Having established the questions on the basis of a research agenda, a methodology had to be devised. On this project it took the following form:

1 a documentary analysis of the curriculum materials (that is, the project packs);
2 interviews with the teachers in the schools, especially the curriculum coordinators and the class teachers;
3 observations of classes, informal conversations with headteachers, teachers and pupils;
4 meetings with all teachers in the schools where the project was being trialled:

      i to discuss the project and their evaluation of it;
     ii to discuss the end of project report prior to its submission.

Accordingly, the project would draw on observational data, interview data obtained from tape recordings and documentary evidence. Even if the project was seen by the local authority to be rubber-stamping their curriculum initiative, for us it was to be a social scientific enquiry in the field of education. However, given the fact that the project had to start on February and a report be delivered by 16 May, fieldwork had to be carefully scheduled. Even more important was the recruitment of a team. The project was only commissioned eleven days before the official start date so a team with the relevant methodological and educational expertise needed to be assembled. The team included: a researcher with case-study experience outside education; a researcher with limited case-study experience within education and who had been a teacher; an educationalist who had vast curriculum experience and myself. Together a set of complementary educational and research skills were available.

There are several lessons to be learned from this experience. First, there is the question of commissioning research with long lead times so that properly equipped research teams can be established. Second, there is the issue of project questions and the extent to which they must be redefined, for without this process cheap consultancy rather than research or evaluation is done. Third, the researcher must consider the way in which an appropriate methodology is established so that reliable and valid data are obtained. Yet even when this is all done, continued care needs to be exercised over the conduct, reporting and use of such studies. While for us the project was a study of curriculum development (Burgess, Candappa, Galloway and Sanday, 1989), for the authority it was an examination of the effectiveness of their materials. Meanwhile, for the local newspaper the focus was the animals discussed in the project. An article in the *Hampshire Chronicle* reported on our study under the headline 'Marwell Zoo is inspiration for project' — a far cry from questions about the operation of the curriculum, race, gender, 'green' issues and the use of qualitative methods.

### Methodological Issues

Central to all research projects is the relationship between the questions that are posed and the methodology that is used. In these circumstances, the methodology needs to be linked to the kinds of questions that are addressed. Accordingly, if we return to the contractor–customer relationship identified by Rothschild, it is not a simple division between those who set the questions and others who answer them. Some consideration must be given to a variety of issues including the time available to conduct the investigation and the way in which the questions can be addressed using a selection or sample of schools. Here, we might turn to studies that have been commissioned in authorities where sufficient money is only available to employ half a researcher for a whole year, yet where the geographical area to be covered is a whole authority. First, we might consider the kinds of questions to be addressed. If we require details of the number of in-service courses organized, the question might be answered through a detailed analysis of the handbook provided by the authority. Such a question may seem deceptively simple, but do we know the balance of courses by age phase, by sector and by topic? Second, LEAs may wish to know who attends courses — an issue that can be addressed by questionnaire design and subsequent analysis. However, if we are to understand the process of in-service education and training, it becomes important to focus on particular events and individuals using participant observation and interview methods. Accordingly, the research issue or question becomes closely linked to the most appropriate methodology.

Having thought the methodology through, access must be gained, but access to what and to whom? Is it that we need to gain access to 'good practice'? This is notoriously difficult to identify, however, given the value-laden judgments associated with notions of good practice. When access is obtained to a selection of events or situations we need to consider what is available. For example, in studying Salford nursery schools and centres we engaged in interviews with headteachers who had no choice but to give us physical access to their schools. However, comments indicated that care had been taken about what was said; as one head remarked: 'I don't think I've said anything controversial and I was worried before [the interview] that I might. I just wonder how I controlled myself!' In turn, physical access may be restricted at institutions where heads have limited where the researchers went or whether they were or were not allowed to remain in the school over the lunch hour.

Similarly, in our studies of in-service education, I have been especially keen to document what occurs on 'Baker days' which involved researchers following the planning and evaluation phases as well as attending the actual days (Burgess *et al.*, 1993). This has on occasion proved difficult, especially in a case where 'nothing' was planned for a Baker day. I considered it important for a researcher to attend so that we know what occurs in such situations, yet at the same time the headteacher concerned wished to persuade the researcher not to visit the school.

Such situations raise a range of ethical issues that link together the sponsorship of the research, the conduct of the inquiry and the subsequent reporting of the study. Central to all the these issues is the identifiability of individuals or groups. Should the researcher protect individuals or groups? Here it might be asked, protection from whom? From themselves? From employers? Or from members of the general public? Second, it raises questions about the ways in which such evidence might subsequently be used either for or against the group that is being studied. For example, in our study of the educational provision for children under five in Salford, we interviewed all the headteachers of nursery schools and centres. A constant question asked by the heads was concerned with the reasons why the study had been commissioned and the implications that might arise from it. In these circumstances, self-interest not just of individuals but also of a whole sector was involved, as the heads were concerned that the outcome of the report might result in radical reorganization of the LEA provision for children under five.

The researcher therefore has a number of considerations with which to grapple in the field and also when writing the report and subsequent papers, presenting feedback and considering the use of such material, as discussed in the next section.

### Reporting Evidence

We probably know least about reporting of all the phases of the research process. In the contractor–customer relationship, however, it is important to know how material is received. In the last year a key aspect of the reporting of projects has involved feedback to sponsors and to those who were part of the studies. Accordingly, evidence will be presented from several projects.

In our study of education for the under-fives in Salford we interviewed all seven nursery centre heads and eleven nursery school heads. When the heads received a copy of the report, great effort was put into identifying individuals in terms of pseudonyms. In addition, note was also taken of the frequency with which named individuals were quoted. In the course of a discussion of the report with the Salford heads, the following comments were made:

Head: When you do look through the report there are a lot of quotes from three or four particular heads and they were all interviewed at the beginning.

RB: How do you know they were interviewed at the beginning?

Head: [amidst laughter] Not only did I identify myself but I could identify everybody else as well.

We were told that headteachers had been calling each other with the pseudonyms that we had used since the report was issued (Burgess, Hughes and Moxon, 1989). Individuals are not always identifiable, however, as we found when we took our energy education report back to Hampshire. Here, one teacher took up an issue raised by a teacher in a quotation in the report. He indicated how he agreed with the comments that had been made by the teacher in the report. The teacher with whom he was in complete agreement was himself (although we did not indicate that this was the case)!

There are other issues concerned with reporting, however. First, there is the extent to which a report is used by a local authority and by headteachers as a check-list. In two projects where we have reported back to LEAs, the actual report has been used as a check-list literally to tick off those areas that the authority has covered. In reporting back on our Salford project on the education of the under-fives, we provided our report in May (just two months after the end of the field-work). However, we were told by one headteacher: 'I think it's a very accurate, extremely accurate picture of how we were at the time we started'. Certainly, such remarks delighted us as researchers but she continued:

Head: I think a lot of it is now out of date already and that's just an example of how fast things are moving already. Most of the criticisms, or what we call criticisms . . . points you wish to make. We have addressed them already so as far as we are concerned we must have been intuitive or something . . .

RB: Can you give me examples of where that has happened? Where we've said something that's now out of date and also examples of where we've said something and it's now different because it's already been done?

Head: Well you did say that it was quite important that we should have a joint system of record keeping, leading to a joint transfer document and before the report came through we had already been on meeting for about two months on that and it's well on the way and the group that's been started by the nursery headteachers includes an educational psychologist, people from nursery classes, from nursery centres, — somebody from the curriculum support team. So it is. Somebody from the planning department so that it does go across the board in as far as we can and that was already done.

> We knew that we had to do it and it's already been
> done.

In these circumstances, it was important to explain that the report
would not be changed and would in its final form recommend a joint
system of record keeping for transfer purposes because we were
reporting things as they were during our study and not how they had
subsequently developed.

On occasion, our attention has been drawn to inaccuracies in our
reports, not in terms of our comments but in terms of those we have
interviewed. For example, we have been shown examples where nursery school heads did not in the view of advisers, have an understanding
of some of the fundamental principles of nursery education. In the case
of one of our reports on in-service education, officers and advisers
discussed the way in which the system was established and operated as
opposed to the way teachers thought it operated.

Such comments have led us to consider the perspective from which
reports are written. We have stressed that our investigations do not
yield 'answers' or need answers. Instead, detailed evidence from case-
study investigations allows us to gain access to the perceptions of individuals who are located at different positions in a local education
authority. Second, it has led us to consider how reports and the evidence contained in those reports might be used.

Some local authorities have indicated that the research may be
used instrumentally with the DES (now DFE) to demonstrate that
some systematic investigation has been conducted in relation to in-
service education and training. In one case, a headteacher used *Educating
the Under-Fives in Salford* to raise a number of questions for his teachers
and governors. He produced a document for them which stated:

> I feel that this piece of work, *Educating the Under-Fives in the
> City of Salford*, [*sic*] is a most comprehensive and searching in-
> vestigation commissioned by the Salford LEA and undertaken
> by the University of Warwick. As a matter of interest, I note
> a number of references to my own contributions, although as
> you will realize, only fictitious names have been used.
>
> There can never be a situation where a school 'gets every-
> thing right all of the time' and I believe that a great benefit
> (no doubt, anticipated by the Authority), is to show the obvious
> wide variation between schools in the various aspects consid-
> ered in the survey [*sic*]. Clearly, this would always be the case
> where headteachers themselves have their own particular notions

of the philosophies of education, where schools make their respective contributions to communities in widely-varying parts of the City and where building constraints and provision of staff vary so greatly.

   The investigation would be worthless if nothing had to be acted upon to a great or less extent.

   Perhaps questions coming to my own mind would illustrate this . . .

Finally, he asked all members of staff to read our report. However, he continued to call our detailed case-study evidence 'a survey' and comments that 'it is much too substantial a document to consider producing additional copies'.

   Such issues have also been raised by local authority officers and advisers who have confused the term 'survey' with 'case-study', the use of interview data with 'observation' and the extent to which the particular relates to more general issues. Our attention also has been drawn to the way in which researchers need to consider the relationship between a summary, a conclusion, recommendations and implications. In particular, our attention has been called to the way in which such evidence might be used by members who might have difficulty with the material in our reports. As one adviser put it, 'I've not got a clue as to the average reading age so they [the members] could have difficulties'. In short, it calls for us to consider carefully how to communicate research evidence.

### Conclusion

At this point we need to reflect upon the relationship between the contractor and the customer and to decide whether or not we should be considering collaborating rather maintaining than a sharp division. What would be the benefits of such collaboration? Here I would wish to point to several areas that we need to explore:

1  The specification of research questions. Here, sharp divisions between the pure and the applied need to be avoided. Instead, ways in which research questions that link to a knowledge base and to policy issues should be addressed.
2  The working out of research methodologies that would be appropriate for the questions posed. Here a number of issues might be considered, such as:

    i   the time scale required,
    ii  the funding possibilities,
    iii the relationship between research questions, funding
        timescales and results.

3 The way in which studies can be conducted, analyzed, reported
  and used — and the creation of appropriate methodologies.
4 The styles of reporting, disseminating and using evidence not
  only among policy-makers, officers and advisers but also among
  teachers.

If these issues become part of our research agenda it will require some
radical rethinking on all sides. No longer will research be a rapidly
commissioned activity with limited funds and short-term goals, nor
will it be abstract and inaccessible. Instead it will begin to point us
towards making links between research and policy and thinking about
long-term projects that are adequately resourced and where we can
begin to consider long-term issues for the benefit of educational practice while simultaneously advancing our knowledge.

## References

BURGESS, R.G., CANDAPPA, M., GALLOWAY, S. and SANDAY, A. (1989) *Energy
    Education and the Curriculum*, Coventry, CEDAR, University of
    Warwick.
BURGESS, R.G., CONNOR, J., GALLOWAY, S., MORRISON, M. and NEWTON, M.
    (1993) *Implementing In-Service Education and Training*, London, Falmer Press.
BURGESS, R.G., HUGHES, C. and MOXON, S. (1989) *Educating the Under-Fives
    in Salford*, CEDAR Reports, No. 1, Coventry, CEDAR, University of
    Warwick.
FINCH, J. (1989) 'Compromises', paper presented to the British Sociological
    Association Annual Conference, Plymouth, April 1989.
HMSO (1971) *A Framework for Government R & D*, London, HMSO.
ROTHSCHILD, LORD (1982) *An Enquiry into the Social Science Research Council*,
    London, HMSO.
SHIPMAN, M. (1988) *The Limitations of Social Research*, 3rd edn, London,
    Longman.

# 3    The Relationship between Educational Research and Evaluation and the Role of the Local Education Authority[1]

*Alan Sanday*

In many ways this chapter is complementary to the previous one, 'Contractors and Customers'. That chapter deals with the relevant issues in general, while this one examines the particular case of the local education authority (LEA) as customer with the university as contractor.

This chapter looks at what is known about the process of decision-making in LEAs, considering the points of contact between this process and educational research and evaluation. This analysis highlights a number of points of tension, which are explored. Finally the chapter relates this to how far the researcher needs to take into account the micropolitics of the LEA in presenting the report.

## The Process of Policy and Decision-Making in LEAs

Although there are some formal descriptions of this process (for example, Jennings, 1977; Bush and Kogan, 1982), an analysis of the micropolitics of an education office would be a valuable addition to the literature. The following description and analysis therefore relies heavily on the personal experience of the author in two LEAs (one county, one city), and conversations with colleagues from other authorities; therefore, its generality cannot be guaranteed.

The first generalization from these experiences is that the process of policy and decision-making is not as linear, logical and systematic as the formal accounts would have us believe. At any point in time an

LEA has under consideration and development an agenda of items. Prior to Sir Keith Joseph as Secretary of State, most of the items on these agendas originated internally in each LEA, and differed considerably between LEAs. Some LEAs gave priority to the development of community education, for example, while with others it might be nursery education or Special Needs; some LEAs were active in many fields, some in few.

The place on the agenda 'for consideration' and eventually the finance for implementation was secured by personal advocacy, often by the Chief Education Officer (CEO), sometimes another senior officer or adviser, or occasionally an elected member. The forum for this advocacy was finally the Education Committee and the Council. The professional reputation of the CEO and the political survival of the Chairman of the Education Committee were therefore intimately and publicly involved in the success of the initiatives they advocated. This is a most important consideration we shall return to later.

Increasingly under Joseph and Baker the agenda for LEAs was set externally by the government. Some of these initiatives were 'voluntary' (but substantially cash-induced), for example, TVEI, LEATGS (GRIST). Others, and more so latterly, were compulsory, for example, comprehensive reorganization, Local Management of Schools (LMS), National Curriculum and Assessment. Even when the initiative is externally imposed, however, the way in which it is implemented within a particular LEA will have been devised by an individual officer or group of officers. Their professional reputations (and possibly their career prospects) will be influenced by the success or otherwise of the strategy selected.

There is in practice a complex interaction between internal and external sources of initiatives. For example, comprehensive education began in certain individual local authorities, the idea originating with one or two chief officers, some of them at least being motivated as much by logistic as educational reasons. Elected members espoused the cause for political reasons; at a political level comprehensive education became government policy and was imposed 'externally' on other LEAs.

This process is not neat, and is influenced little or not at all by educational research and evaluation. An educational researcher might have hoped for a 'clean' pilot project in which the changes in a carefully selected group of schools were evaluated against some clearly enunciated aims, for example, to improve the educational attainments of all abilities, to improve the access of middle and lower socio-economic groups to higher education. The time-scale for 'clean' educational research is much longer than that for politics, and the only hope for intervention would have been by a 'quick and dirty' evaluation of one of the early projects — an evaluation of a kind with which few educational researchers would have wished to have been associated. Thus the scope for research and evaluation is thereby diminished; it is reduced to discovering how comprehensive education might be improved—banding v. mixed ability, core v. options.

It has to be said, however, that even if there had been a 'quick and dirty' evaluation, the nature of the decision-making process is such that the results might well have been ignored. Political decision-making results from advocacy, not a careful weighing of the evidence. It is difficult for an advocate to surrender his or her cause, whatever the evidence, without commiting professional or political suicide.

This process is now about to be repeated with respect to the 1988 Education Reform Act. There is no evidence that a system of assessment of the kind proposed will bring about an improvement in the effectiveness of schools, and no evidence is being sought. 'As we have seen, there is little evidence that the introduction of testing raises standards short of teaching to the test' (Gipps, 1990, p. 34). The role of the educational research establishment is reduced to finding ways in which assessment can be implemented with the least damaging effects. Similarly, with respect to LMS, Martin Leonard in the Times Educational Supplement (21.9.90) writes:

> The pace of change is itself part of the problem, in addition to causing difficulties for outside observers. The introduction of LMS could have been managed in such a way as to avoid most of the difficulties which now beset it. There could have been genuine pilot projects — and it should be remembered that not even the Cambridgeshire project was close enough to the rules laid down in the 88 Act to count as a true pilot. The pilots could have covered both formula-funding and local management, with control groups and careful evaluation: they could have investigated the expected problem areas, particularly information systems and the consequences of having a salary scale with automatic increments. But all this would have taken time, which, for political reasons, was not available.

Our description so far of the process of decision-making in LEAs has spotlighted two major potential tensions:

1 the shortness of the political time-scale compared to the research time-scale, and

2 the way in which the success of particular developments to be evaluated is related to the personal advocacy of officers and elected members.

A third potential point of tension concerns the way in which evaluation and research are financed by LEAs. Even before the days of LMS and the delegation of the majority of the budget to schools, by far the majority of an LEA budget was pre-empted by major items such as salaries, and the proportion of disposable finance is very small. Under LMS the proportion of the budget disposable by the centre is drastically reduced. Therefore in LEA terms evaluation is very expensive. Thus when initiatives are conceived within individual authorities (such as community education, Records of Achievement, COMPACT, modular curriculum), it is seldom that a budget for evaluation is included in the funding. It frequently occurs that initiatives are perpetuated and even disseminated nationally before even rudimentary evaluation.

A recent and important example is school self-evaluation as an instrument for improving the effectiveness of schools. In the late 1970s and early 80s a number of LEAs (Solihull and Oxfordshire, among others) developed various forms of school self-evaluation. Before any evaluation was commissioned or published, self-evaluation was widely advocated and became a prominent feature of most school improvement projects (like GRIDS). When an evaluation by researchers at the Open University was eventually published (Clift, Nuttall and McCormick, 1987) the limitations of self-evaluation were dramatically exposed. Again the length of the research time-scale was an important factor. Furthermore, since the time-scale for the dissemination of research is even longer, there is a danger that unmodified forms of self-evaluation will become a feature of many processes for formulating school development plans despite the strictures of the Open University researchers.

Although it is seldom, if ever, treated systematically, policies are in competition with each other for funding at the time each LEA carries out its Annual Review of Expenditure (a process now complicated even further by Local Management of Schools). The question being asked implicitly is: In order to improve the effectiveness of the schools, what is the best mix of expenditure on teachers, ancilliaries, support services, community education, etc.? For example, some LEAs have sometimes been criticized for spending too much on support services like Special Needs Support Teams and advisers, rather than teachers in classrooms, but what evidence is there as to which is the more effective in improving performance? In order to answer these questions and improve cost effectiveness, far more extensive evaluations are required than are available. In practice the question is usually answered implicitly by reference to custom within the authority, external constraints such as government-specific funding, and the personal advocacy of individual officers and members.

Our description and analysis of the process of decision-making in LEAs has yielded at least three important insights:

1  Decision-making needs to be informed by much more research and evaluation than is at present available, but this is unlikely to happen because the disposable finance available to an LEA centrally is already small and will be further drastically diminished by LMS.

2  The time-scale for research is long compared to that for policy-making and action with the result that developments are often disseminated before they have been adequately evaluated, for example, self-evaluation of schools as a tool for improving effectiveness.

3  Developments in an LEA are usually the result of personal advocacy by an officer and elected members.

The important corollary to this is that the LEA will be unable to digest an evaluation which appears to be critical. One of the few circumstances under which this acceptance might be possible would be if the receipt of the critical evaluation fortuitously coincided with a change of staff. Although under LMS (and 'opting out') much of the decision-making will be transferred to the level of the school, much the same strictures apply.

### Points of Contact between Research/Evaluation and LEAs

The main points of contact are:

1  Through the generalized dissemination of research findings by periodicals such as *the Times Educational Supplement and Education* (Caplan, Morrison and Stambaugh, 1975; Nisbet and Broadfoot, 1980).

The effect is to 'create an agenda of concern' which is taken up selectively by individual officers, advisers and elected members.
For example, when the Bennett work on teaching methods

in primary schools was first published, some Education Committees were stimulated to ask for a report on teaching methods in their own schools, and more recently some Committees have been excited by the media reports on reading standards and methods ('phonics', 'look and say' and 'real books'). Clearly this gives great (undue?) importance to the selectivity exercised by journalists, and it has been debated whether there ought to be a more systematic way of supplying an abstract of information.

A major impediment, to which we shall be repeatedly referring, is that few LEAs have a systematic mechanism for the digestion and dissemination of such information. A notable exception was the Research and Statistics branch of the ILEA (now disbanded). The situation has now become even more difficult because under the 88 Act much of this information is required at the level of governors as well as LEA officers.

2   DES/HMI surveys and reviews.

Of recent years these have become more numerous and extensive. Potentially they are a significant source of some of the information needed by LEAs, but again their value is diminished because few LEAs methodically absorb them into the system.

However there are some important differences in methodology between these and the work of 'academic' evaluators (Finch, 1986, p. 69). In the 1978 HMI report *Primary Education in England* an important conclusion concerns the alleged mismatch between teachers' expectations of children and their capabilities. It appears that this conclusion was drawn from observations by HMI over two days in each school, reporting on a five-point scale ranging from 'considerable over-expectation' to 'considerable under-expectation'. (We do not know what steps if any were taken to ensure that all HMI used the same criteria). The report then proceeds to treat this exercise in professional judgment as hard fact.

To many academic evaluators this would seem a flawed methodology. They would have expected at least some objective measure of pupil capability, a written teacher rating of capability, and some statistical measure of the divergence. Now it may be of course that there would be a strong correlation between the results of both methodologies, in which case the

HMI methodology is the more efficient in terms of the expenditure of time. Considering how often 'professional judgment' is used its reliability compared with more conventional but time-consuming methods would repay more research.

3   Internally commissioned research and evaluation.

Most LEAs employ professional staff from whom surveys and evaluations can be commissioned. The most notable example in Britain was the Research and Statistics Division of ILEA, but most LEAs have advisers/inspectors on whom they can call.

The advantages of using these are:

— the evaluation is not an additional expense;
— they are well aware of the context in which the results of the evaluation must be delivered;
— their length of experience, perceptiveness and judgment compare very favourably with that of staff likely to be available from other sources.

The disadvantages of using them are:

— the nature of their other duties are such that it is difficult to release them for this purpose;
— they have probably not been trained in evaluation techniques;
— they are likely to have been concerned with the implementation of the projects they are evaluating;
— in some circumstances they may feel constrained by the need to preserve long-term relationships;
— because of the wide variety of audiences for their reports, they will probably feel constrained to a reporting style which is opaque and requires 'decoding'.

4   Externally commissioned evaluation.

In LEA terms, externally commissioned evaluation is very expensive (see above), and it is unlikely to happen unless a budget for it is mandatorily included in an externally funded project. A discussion of external evaluations follows.

Initially when an LEA approaches a research institution, it is probably not because they are clear about what evaluation they need, but because they have been told they must have some external evaluation! The LEA will therefore probably need some help in clarifying its needs, and this must be done carefully. Otherwise the LEA expectations will change and become more demanding during the course of the evaluation in ways which researchers will find difficult to meet. An additional complication is that, as was pointed out above, many LEAs do not have a clear and consistent point of contact and the researcher may be floating between, say, an administrator and the Chief Adviser (who may or may not enjoy the best of professional relationships with each other).

The first expectation of the LEA will be an expertise which they do not have themselves. This in itself may raise difficulties for the providing institution, because although they may have a generalized research expertise, they may not have the permanent staff to accumulate specific expertise in a rapidly changing field, on assessment, for example. There may well be someone on the LEA advisory staff who has considerably more specific knowledge than anyone in the evaluation team.

The evaluation supervisor knows that this is not relevant because the methodology to be employed does not rely on specific 'professional judgment' in the manner in which this is used by LEA inspectors (see above). The essence of the qualitative method is the collection and analysis of comments from participants, and the skill of the researcher lies in eliciting insightful and representative comments. However this distinction may not be clear to LEA staff and to teachers.

The second difficulty for the providing institution is recruiting appropriately qualified staff and training them during the lifetime of the project. The third difficulty is providing adequate supervision. Some LEAs have unfortunate experiences when they commission an evaluation from a 'famous name' who provides grossly inadequate supervision to poorly trained researchers. It is possible that in many cases the researchers will be considerably shorter on school experience than the LEA staff. As with specific subject knowledge, this is not relevant to the research methodology to be employed, but it gives the LEA and teachers an opportunity to 'rubbish' the conclusions if these are not acceptable (see below).

There is always the danger (?) that during the course of the evaluation the evaluator becomes an advocate. This may be very acceptable to some (but not necessarily all) in the LEA, but the evaluator must be aware of how far the evaluation might be compromised in the eyes of some audiences.

All evaluation makes demands on already overworked teachers, and unless care is taken to convince them of the benefits (preferably to them) of the evaluation there is a danger of an increasing credibility gap (based on the lack of 'professional expertise' of the evaluators) and declining cooperation. In any case the methodology should always be designed to make minimum demands on teachers.

In the end, if not in the beginning, LEA expectations are likely to be 'hard nosed'. For example, on INSET, LEAs must answer questions such as

1   What is the best way of matching provision to need: a central programme, allocation of finance to advisers, allocation of finance to schools?
2   What is the most effective and least disruptive method of provision?
3   How should priorities be determined?

A considerable tension may result if researchers feel that a much more extensive evaluation would be required to answer questions such as these, and the LEA feels that the evaluation already done should have provided more answers to the questions it is compelled to answer.

The researcher/evaluator is always aware that there are at least two audiences — the LEA and the academic world. Thus as well as being interested in the actual evaluation, the researcher may be interested in (and wish later to write about) what the exercise contributes to the development of evaluation technique. This can be seen to be legitimate from every point of view, since it is desirable that each one-off evaluation should contribute something to the generalized theoretical framework on which all evaluations draw. This is, after all, the one strength of what the university has to offer. However this may not always be clear to LEAs who in some cases may have felt that the researcher is more interested in academic publication for his or her own aggrandisement, and that the LEA is being used (or abused) for this purpose.

Another point of tension may be rights of publication. The researcher may well think that they have been clarified in the initial contract, but at that stage the LEA may feel that it is a matter of little importance. However if the final report contains material which the LEA considers derogatory, it may well wish to renege on the contract!

The final problem for the researchers, and a most important one, is how to present the results. One aspect is the question of the length of the report. Maybe many researchers, and clients, have a gut feeling that a substantial research grant demands a substantial report — perhaps one kilogram per £5,000? Never mind the quality, feel the weight! On the other hand, the brutal truth is that there is probably no one in the LEA to whom the report is anywhere near as important as it is to the researcher, and the LEA probably has no way of digesting a voluminous report. The best solution to this dilemma appears to be to commence the report with a summary on two or three sides of standard A4 paper *well cross-referenced to the evidence in the main text.* It will then be possible for a large number of people to read the summary and follow up in the main text just those parts of most concern to themselves.

By far the most important aspect of reporting is how the conclusions will react with the micropolitics of the LEA. Let us consider an LEA where, largely on the initiative of the Chief Adviser, schools have been encouraged to carry out a self-evaluation as a means of formulating their INSET needs. This process has been evaluated by an in-depth study of one school. The evaluator concluded that for a variety of reasons the strategy was not effective (Clift *et al.*, 1987, p. 190) — conflict of purpose, 'professional threat' perceived by teachers, overload, the tediousness of the process.

The Chief Adviser and the head may well feel their professional credibility attacked by this conclusion — the Chief Adviser as the initiator of the strategy, and the head teacher who feels that it is implied that the strategy ought to have worked had he carried it out more competently.

A researcher pitching an evaluation into this situation might anticipate several possible reactions. An adverse evaluation might be rubbished by disparaging the researchers (Less than three years as a researcher? Not enough experience! More than three years experience? Too long out of schools — lost touch!). Another ploy is for the receivers to seize on one fairly innocuous recommendation which is discussed at great length and finally adopted so that all the more important recommendations can be avoided. Or the researchers might be given the 'ignore them' treatment — meetings repeatedly postponed, or attended only by a few individuals of obviously low status. Of course this may happen by accident rather than design, since the evaluation is often far less significant to the LEA than to the researcher who did it.

A very important question then is this: how far should the way in which the report might be received be a concern of the researcher in presenting the findings? If the report is presented with an attitude of 'take it or leave it', a year or more of work may be consigned to oblivion, but if the presentation regards the micropolitics of the LEA would the researcher feel that integrity had been compromised?

## Conclusions

For their process of decision-making, LEAs (and schools) need to have available to them much more research and evaluation. In particular they need to be able to get rapid evaluations of initiatives as they develop; this should have happened with both self-evaluation of schools and modular curriculum. Otherwise there is the danger that much effort and money will be wasted, and even positive damage perpetrated, in disseminating seriously flawed initiatives. Conversely, as a backlash, the beneficial content of an initiative may be lost. In other words, if it had been refined by evaluation at an early stage it might have worked.

With the advent of LMS the finance available to LEAs for evaluation purposes is minute, and no individual LEA is in a position to replicate the dismantled ILEA Research and Statistics Branch. What would be the prospects for regional cooperative arrangements involving universities as contractors? The mistrust which frequently exists among LEAs themselves, and LEA mistrust of university research, would be major obstacles, and opting-out is not a propitious climate.

A third point is that ways would have to be found of adapting the time-scale or evaluation to the short time-scale of development of policy-making.

Finally, there needs to be extensive discussion prior to evaluation as to how the various possible results, especially 'adverse' results, might be handled.

## Note

1  Since this chapter was written, the finance available to LEAs to commission research and evaluation has decreased even further, mainly due to the impact of LMS. Nevertheless, the issues are still relevant to the decreased agenda or to the 'contractor–customer' relationship.

## References

BUSH, T. and KOGAN, M. (1982) *Directors of Education*, London, George Allen and Unwin.

CAPLAN, N., MORRISON, A. and STANBAUGH, R. (1975) *The Use of Social Science Knowledge in Policy Decisions at National Level*, Ann Arbor, MI, University of Michigan.

CLIFT, P., NUTTALL, D. and McCORMICK, R. (Eds) (1987) *Studies in School Self-Evaluation*, London, Falmer Press.

DES (1978) *Primary Education in England: A Survey by HMI of Schools*, London, HMSO.

FINCH, J. (1986) *Research and Policy*, Lewes, Falmer Press.

GIPPS, C. (1990) *Assessment: A Teacher's Guide to the Issues*, London, Hodder and Stoughton.

JENNINGS, R. (1977) *Education and Politics*, London, Batsford.

LEONARD, M. (1990) *Times Educational Supplement*.

MAGEE, B. (1973) *Popper*, London, Fontana.

McMAHON, A. *et al.* (1984) *Guidelines for Review and Internal Development of Schools (GRIDS)*, York, Longmans.

MORTIMORE, P. *et al.* (1988) *School Matters*, London, Open Books.

NISBET, J. and BROADFOOT, P. (1980) *The Impact of Research on Policy and Practice in Education*, Aberdeen, Aberdeen University Press.

RUTTER, M. *et al.* (1979) *Fifteen Thousand Hours*, London, Open Books.

# 4 Educational Evaluations for the US Congress: Some Reflections on Recent Experience[1]

*Eleanor Chelimsky and Frederick Mulhauser*

## Introduction

This chapter has two purposes. The first is to sketch for an international audience the complex structure within which educational policy and practice come alive in the United States, and to give one view of the current major issues and dilemmas now facing education in the United States. The second is to report on program evaluation in education as practiced by the General Accounting Office (GAO) for our major audience, the US Congress. Towards that end, the chapter describes GAO's recent work on urban education and the problems of arguably the most vulnerable children in the US, with three studies as examples. The chapter concludes with a look at the resources for inquiry in education in the US, and recent work by GAO which had an impact in increasing those resources.

## The Context for Educational Evaluation in the US

The United States educational system is big, decentralized and subject to innumerable competing influences and definitions of purpose. Enrollment in US schools includes (in 1988) 45.9 million in pre-college or the first twelve years, and another 12.5 million in higher education, for a total of over 58 million.[2] That is almost exactly the same as the entire population of the United Kingdom.

'Lower' education — the first twelve years — comprises 16,000 local public school districts each with a governing board. (Only about one out of nine of American youth in this age group attend non-public schools). The most salient demographic facts are that almost one-third of the US school population is now minority, over 40 per cent of both black and Hispanic children live in poverty, and such students are strongly concentrated in central cities.

As they provide half the money to run the schools, the fifty states retain strong leverage over schools, through their own apparatus of boards and administrators. Local taxes are second most important; the national government provides only 6 per cent (though even in earlier times, compared to the current decline, the federal share was only up to 10 per cent). About $4,000 (or £2,500) is spent, on average, yearly per child in US schools, though there is great variation around the country, from $2,350 (or £1,468) in Mississippi to $6,500 (£4,062) in New York.

Beyond the twelfth year of schooling, the US system of higher or post-secondary education is somewhat more diverse than the pre-college system, including 3,000 colleges and universities offering two-year and four-year programs as well as graduate studies. In addition there are thousands more vocational schools. Public (tax-supported) institutions, governed at state, county, or lower levels, predominate, though not as much as in K–12 schooling, sharing enrolment with private colleges and universities in a ratio of 3 to 1. Minority student enrolment at this level lags substantially behind that of white students of the same age (18 and 22 per cent for Hispanic and black youth respectively, compared to 28 per cent for white). Part-time attendance at two-year colleges has been the major growth in recent years.

US education policy and practice, therefore, includes a great range of institutions dealing with varying mixes of students, working towards diverse educational aims, directed in a formal sense by a great variety of public and private sources of finance and governance, not to mention subject to myriad other influences from students, parents, employers, teachers, and the public at large. This complexity makes it challenging just to get accurate data on practice and outcomes in US education, let alone to establish some problems as most important and pursue remedies consistently.

In the 1980s, education, especially the pre-college level, has sustained a major growth of public attention. Governors and legislatures in many states in the mid-1980s actively reviewed their schools' funding and performance, reflecting growing awareness of the link between states' economic health and the educational attainments of their workforce. Federal legislation had proliferated earlier, in the period

1965–1980, but increasing budget limits (the combined effect of tax cuts and the priority placed on enhancing defense) and a rather conservative view of the appropriate central government role have combined to reduce federal initiative since then. Exhortation has been a major method of influence. A federal report stimulated much of the state review,[3] and one visible and articulate Secretary of Education, William J. Bennett, drew significant public attention to education through aggressive addresses from the pulpit of his post. The candidates in the 1988 presidential election gave unprecedented attention to education, and President George Bush selected education as one major domestic policy emphasis. The major effort by President Bush to influence education has been to convene state governors and to develop with them a set of ambitious national education goals including improvement in both the environment of schools and the students' achievements.

## GAO's Role and Selected Major Issues in Education

GAO is a legislative agency, established to provide independent data and analysis for the US Congress. The Program Evaluation and Methodology Division (PEMD), in particular, applies state-of-the-art research and evaluation methods to examine the effects of current policies, the probable effects of proposed initiatives, and the quality of policymaking information. The division has a staff of about 100 with perhaps sixty studies under way at any time. The division, like all of GAO, communicates results in varied ways including reports, testimony, briefings, and recently in the form of special video presentations shown over the congressional closed-circuit television system. Specific reports are directed to congressional requestors for the most part, but may also be addressed to heads of executive branch departments. GAO makes recommendations based on its findings (which by law must be responded to if they are addressed to a department), and also aggressively tracks for several years whether the recommendations are acted upon.

The GAO role is typically to review executive branch actions, including auditing financial systems, and in program areas, reviewing evaluations. That is, we would not usually ourselves perform either routine audits or evaluations, but would examine the soundness of such work in a systemic sense. However, in recent years, the marked decline in evaluations by the executive agencies has forced us to do more of them ourselves.[4]

From our review of education in the United States, including consultation with a panel of experienced educators and observers, we

*Table 4.1: Major educational policy questions for GAO emphasis, 1988–92*

1  How can the need be met for expanded pre-school education services in sufficient quantity and of appropriate quality?
2  Have the elementary and secondary schools improved their ability to increase the competitiveness of the United States in a world economy that is increasingly dominated by technological applications?
3  How can we ensure the supply and quality of the teaching force in the public schools?
4  What is the cause and what are potential remedies for the increasingly unsuccessful performance of large city school systems?
5  The education of the disadvantaged may have been neglected as a result of federal budget cutting and the recent focus upon educational reform throughout elementary and secondary schools. What has been the impact of this trend on the educational opportunities of disadvantaged youth?
6  To what degree has the evaluation of the effectiveness of federal programs been threatened by widespread breaches of proper educational testing procedures?
7  Why has the rate of minority enrolment and graduation from college been declining in recent years and what can be done to reverse this decline?

identified in 1987 seven major issues (shown in Table 4.1) on which to concentrate if we were to be of most use to Congress in the period 1988–92. Education decision-makers closer to the school and class-room level would no doubt have different agendas of key items for evaluation and analysis, or would view the same topics differently.

The list reflects a number of aspects of the current debates on education in the United States. First, there is wide agreement (agreement aided enormously by some powerful effects shown by longitud-inal evaluation data) that early schooling is an effective way to forestall later problems.[5] Legislation to expand one approach, called the Head Start program, has been passed in the last year, but there remains great uncertainty among other means, and we would like to contribute to the debate whatever can be learned about how to expand such services efficiently and effectively. One option would be to create new service delivery programs (with a major uncertainty being the proper location — in schools or elsewhere?) which would permit administrative con-trol over the offerings and staff, but others favor simply giving tax credits to parents who enrol their children in pre-school.

Our second priority concerns education's relation to competitive-ness and how schools are preparing youth to lead and respond to changes in work, especially the rise of technology. The age-old debate con-tinues over the purposes of education and the definition of an 'educated person' (shown by the huge popularity of two books on 'what every-one should know', by professors Bloom and Hirsch),[6] but the matter has been chiefly resolved by policy-makers in search of funds (at the state level especially in recent years) by appeal to highly instrumental economic-development goals. These goals set an agenda for educators, and for those who would evaluate the effectiveness of their work, to monitor work skills needed and whether schools impart them.

Our third priority will lead us to studies of the teacher workforce. Current concern for teacher quality stems from the paradox that in the United States, women's opportunities in other career fields have expanded dramatically, hence schoolteaching with its lower income and modest promotion potential no longer commands consideration by such a large pool of able graduates. Instead, it turns out that the men and women choosing education careers are among the lowest achievers in the university, which is worrisome in general but especially as the need expands for sound teaching of technical fields, math and science, and for teaching complex, higher-order skills in all fields.[7]

The fourth and fifth priorities call for us to attend to historic concerns of federal education policy for the most vulnerable students, the largely poor and minority children of the cities. In another paradox of our history, the desegregation of suburban housing since World War II has permitted some urban minority families to move out in search of space and opportunity. Yet the same movement has left behind fragmented communities and marginal, incomplete families barely able to survive economically, let alone to nurture children in a milieu of enormously needy citizens, shrinking jobs for low-skilled persons, and overburdened governments. Educational challenges are especially severe in American cities now, and evaluation should locate whatever rays of hope can be found in promising practices.

Work on the sixth issue will lead us to look into the possible corruption of the basic indicators of schooling outcomes. The United States educational system has a dual view of tests, a love–hate relationship which has resulted in both their widespread use and continual attacks on them from every conceivable vantage-point. The fringe attacks stress such points as the psychic dulling said to result from multiple-choice questions. More reasonably, in recent years there has been renewed attention to the fairness of standardized tests, to the importance of including essay as well as multiple-choice questions, to the relevance of nationally-published tests to what is taught in the decentralized school systems, and to their restrictive influence on instruction when scores serve, European-style, as rationing devices for individuals or as indicators (such as to legislators) that schooling is going well or poorly for groups. For GAO's congressional clients there is a particular interest in testing for federal policy, as scores on nationally-standardized achievement tests (formally administered by local schools and developed by private firms) are aggregated and used as indicators in assessing effects of special federal programs.

The seventh issue brings us to higher education. The federal role in United States higher education comprises a wide range of programs including sponsoring most of the nation's basic biomedical and other scientific research, giving tax advantages to gifts to schools, regulating the institutions directly such as on civil rights and animal rights, and offering grants and loans directly to students. The federal role with respect to students is said to have two goals, enhancing basic access to advanced schooling but also increasing students' choices among the institutions providing it. We selected as our seventh topic that of access for minorities. Both equity and the future needs of the country for a more and more educated workforce suggest that we cannot be satisfied with a situation in which, for example, despite an increase in the young adult black population, blacks earned fewer degrees in 1985 than in 1977. Only 13.6 per cent of the black population aged 25–29 in 1987 had completed four years of college, while the proportion for Hispanics was 14.7 per cent. About double that proportion of whites had the equivalent amount of education.[8]

This framework has served as a set of priorities to inform our discussions with legislators and staff in the last few years. GAO does its work either at the specific request of a committee chair (or sometimes individual members) in Congress, or at our own initiative, though request work predominates. Having a well-grounded set of priorities helps in choosing among the many requests for GAO work and insures that we contribute to the most pressing education topics.

### Three PEMD Education Evaluations

By their requests, Members of Congress have selected the fourth and fifth issues in our list as most important — those dealing with disadvantaged students and urban schools. Three recent studies in this area will illustrate some of the evaluation purposes, users and types in PEMD's work, as well as some dilemmas and unique frailties of evaluation work in education.

The topics of the three studies and the central question in each are as follows:

- Education reform: when states recently increased school-graduation standards, did that create problems for at-risk students who were already having trouble in school?
- Bilingual education: what is known about the effectiveness of different ways of teaching students who come to school knowing little English?

- Urban schools: how promising are certain private voluntary efforts to 'adopt' disadvantaged urban youngsters at an early age and change their educational motivation by guaranteeing them college tuition as well as support along the way?

*The Effects of Education Reform*

This study arose from a committee's interest in vocational education, a very large federal program that required a legislative extension and revision. Many states had responded to the critique of schools' results by increasing basic academic courses required for graduation, adding new required tests and related remedial work, and requiring certain grades for participation in activities. Our congressional requestors wondered if such higher standards had posed problems for students already on the edge of school failure, had perhaps reduced opportunity to study vocational topics, further reduced academic performance, or even increased rates of school-leaving.

In terms of a framework outlined elsewhere for analyzing evaluations, this study was for policy formulation purposes. That is, we aimed to help legislative users judge a situation and decide whether federal action might be needed to enhance opportunities for a particular group of students. The major user was a legislative authorizing committee (not one that allocates funds). The type of study was an impact evaluation, as it assessed how certain state requirements, implemented in local schools, affected students.[9]

Using extensive computer data files from four cities, we examined the achievement test scores (reading and math in each of four cities, for eight comparisons total), attendance and course enrolment transcripts of 61,000 students, representing distinct cohorts or groups passing through high school immediately before and just after the reforms. We separated students who were already poor in reading comprehension in eighth grade, as well as minority students, for analysis as the populations 'at risk'.

We told the congressional requestors that their basic fears had not materialized. Disadvantaged students appear to have improved performance in three of the eight comparisons. However the improvements were modest and there were no signs of improvement in the five other cases. (Teaching to the test may have caused the gains, so even the small rises observed may or may not have been educationally significant.) Black students did about the same as low-achieving students in each city; only Hispanic students failed to share in the few gains we did find. Although disadvantaged students did not experience dramatic improvements, they were not excluded from the gains accruing to the nondisadvantaged. Indeed, in our study sites the latter were no more likely than disadvantaged students to show signs of improvement.

Impacts on school-leaving proved hard to judge, because of the lack of good data, but in the two districts where we had them we found the effects were mixed and the same for all students. We saw a slight decline in vocational course enrolments, but not so great as the increase in other classes, as districts expanded the day to permit taking the other newly-required classes.[10]

*Methods of Teaching Non-English-Speaking Students*

This study brought us into the supercharged area of language and politics, with a focus on the educational subset of questions about how the majority society ought to treat language minorities. Our work was again requested by a legislative authorizing committee and had a clearer link to past and proposed federal policy than in the previous example.

In this case, the Secretary of Education in 1985 took a highly visible position against a longstanding federal program (still in effect) that sponsors school programs for students with limited English. The program required that the native language be used to the extent necessary. The program is voluntary, for those who were willing to apply for the funds and, if selected, to abide by the language requirements set down in the law. However, the program served as a notice that to some degree the federal government endorsed such native-language instruction, a proposition increasingly questioned on various grounds in recent years.

The Secretary proposed elimination of the native-language teaching provision, buttressing his proposal with firm citation of 'accumulated research' on the ineffectiveness of the approach (in contrast to claimed promising evaluations of other methods such as those in French Canada where English-speaking students are immersed in French and receive little or no help in their native language). The request to GAO was for what the staff called 'an intellectual audit', which we understood to mean an assessment of the department's reading of the evidence. The larger purpose was to allow the committee to reach an independent judgment on the department's claim that to continue the requirement would be to continue a 'bankrupt course' and to 'throw good money after bad'.

We agreed only to consider the research and evaluation evidence on teaching methods' effectiveness for limited English pupils, not on other key questions such as the feasibility of different methods. The type of study was a synthesis, rather than new data-collection, as the existing literature on language learning and language instruction in school is very large. However, time constraints precluded doing a new synthesis ourselves. Thus we used existing reviews of the literature, after extensive search and screening for quality, to represent what is known, and used an expert panel to assess the match between that literature and the department's statements. The panel was chosen very carefully to include members with a range of knowledge including the obvious language teaching and learning topics, but also social science study design and cumulation methods. In addition six of ten panel members were recommended by the department, had been cited by them, or had been used as senior consultants.

We reported to Congress that by and large the expert panel disagreed with the department on how to interpret the accumulated research in this area.[11] The panel, with some exceptions, believed that the law's existing requirement (that sponsored programs should use children's native language 'to the extent necessary') had a sound foundation in language-learning research and in evaluation of programs. Furthermore, the panel did not read the evidence for alternatives nearly as favorably as did the Secretary, and thought the Canadian situation too different to permit generalization of the favorable results obtained there.

## Tuition Guarantees to Spur Student Motivation

The third study concerns the longstanding question of what sorts of incentives will change disadvantaged students' motivation to apply themselves to school studies and persist in the longer and longer period of schooling now required to assure a high-wage job. The specific request once again was for the purpose of assisting policy formulation by a legislative committee facing the revision of the federal programs aiding access to higher education. In this case the activity to be studied was not federal, nor even state or local. GAO was asked to look at certain private-sector efforts in which individuals and groups have 'adopted' or selected for sponsorship disadvantaged youngsters at an early age, offering tuition guarantees and supportive services across five or more years in hopes of thereby preventing the familiar pattern of meager school enthusiasm and equally modest results.

In terms of study type, the work was in part what we call front-end analysis, reviewing for decision-makers the assumptions, theories, and alternative goals of the private-sector programs. This displayed a range of possible directions for federal efforts. Since most of the programs we found are quite new, these private-sector programs are best seen as a stimulus for further thinking and design of alternatives rather than a source of proven results.

There is also an element of evaluability analysis in our work. Again, because of the programs' youth and because their aim is to attain their impact across a half-dozen years, outcome evaluation is premature. We did, however, note that the modest data now being maintained will not permit strong evaluation conclusions to be drawn in future on the programs' various goals of school retention, school performance, and further education beyond grade 12.

We found at the outset of the work that few data now exist that could permit synthesis, and that the projects were scattered and not even aware of each other. Our work, therefore, started with the most basic task of assembling a master list of tuition guarantee projects. (We used 'snowball' telephone canvassing techniques starting from references we found in a computer search of a national computerized newspaper and magazine database seeking articles announcing sponsorship programs or citing the inspiration of certain well-publicized figures.) We then surveyed all the projects we found, and visited six projects that represented different approaches to the tuition-guarantee and sponsorship.

We concluded (and titled our report to show our main message) that, in their most intense form, the tuition guarantee and personal sponsorship efforts were indeed promising, considering both their plausible design features (emphasizing considerable hours of additional instruction, among others) and their early success in keeping youth in school. We found one example of programs of this type in operation long enough to show results, including enormously improved completion and continuation rates for those involved compared to rates for other youth from the neighborhoods not given the intense assistance. We used our survey data to characterize the wide range of programs across the country, and the site visit observations to highlight issues such efforts face. We addressed costs and barriers to replication, to aid the legislators in considering public, expanded versions of such programs. Because of the small amount of outcome evidence, however, we did not recommend any specific action at this time, though we did strongly urge the programs to continue evaluation in view of the likelihood of results and we provided a short guide to how such evaluation could

Table 4.2:   *Characteristics of three GAO education evaluations*

| Study | Evaluation Purpose | User(s) | Type of Study |
|---|---|---|---|
| Education reform | Policy formulation | Legislative authorizing committee | Impact evaluation |
| Bilingual education | Policy formulation; accountability | Legislative authorizing committee; agency officials | Synthesis |
| Tuition guarantees | Policy formulation | Legislative authorizing committee | Front-end analysis; evaluability assessment |

best be designed as an appendix to our report (which went back to all those we visited and surveyed, as well as to the congressional requestors).[12] Table 4.2 summarizes all three projects on dimensions of evaluation purpose, user(s), and type of study.

## What Have We Learned from PEMD's Evaluation Work in Education?

Two durable general points emerge across our education work. First, is the inescapability of politics — a perennial observation or complaint of evaluators, but especially acute for us in our education work since by and large we find legislators eager for sound analyses of the sort we are well-equipped to provide.[13] This is despite the long tradition of federal support for education evaluation, including legislatively mandated studies going back to James Coleman's On Equality of Educational Opportunity survey in 1965, and a sophisticated early example of a federal agency evaluation division starting in the 1960s under John Evans within the former US Office of Education (the predecessor of the cabinet-level Department of Education that was created in 1979).

In two cases of completed studies we reported, education reform and bilingual education, political pressures led to our analyses being less useful than we hoped. In the case of our work on education reform, we saw small effects from the states' increased graduation requirements (with especially weak outcomes for Hispanic students, whose academic slide was hardly halted by the reformed requirements) and we noted the possibility that simply teaching to the test had produced the few effects we did see. (Research of others suggests that schools are also simply relabelling courses so that they appear to meet the new requirements, without any change of what is taught or how.) Our results got small attention, either at federal or other levels. The congressional hearing we addressed was on the federal vocational education law; because our finding on the decline in vocational courses was undramatic, perhaps that explained the small discussion of our other results, which would have brought the committee into general discussions of the states' reforms and the likely effects of alternative improvement strategies on the overall health of education — topics well beyond the focus on the specific vocational education program under consideration. At the state level also, we saw little discussion of our work after the testimony and report. We speculate that there are strong incentives to continue the regulatory approach to school improvement that the higher graduation requirements represent. The need will continue for state officials to appear to be *somehow* dealing with educational problems, and the effective symbolism of 'raising standards' may gain political rewards quite apart from evidence such as ours and others' of modest effects.[14]

In the case of bilingual education the central issue we were asked to address, the effectiveness of alternative teaching methods, was transformed. Political realities reframed the policy debate and made our evaluation question less salient. Press and participants reported to us that few legislative leaders were willing to advocate for the bilingual program and claim its effectiveness, as that would risk a charge of encouraging linguistic separatism. (Such a charge, in our view, misstates the goals of bilingual educators, the organized language minority groups, and most parents and students.)

When the legislative work on this program ended, non-native-language teaching approaches were more eligible for funds than before, and the key data were not on what teaching approach might be best but rather on the thin concentrations of many language groups which, school officials claim, make it impossible to find native-language teachers.[15] Such schools argued that they should be able to get federal funds for alternative teaching methods for limited-English students without being held to a requirement of using native language. This viewpoint was widespread, and when buttressed by other kinds of data on the concentrations of language minorities (in fact, data provided by another GAO division), was persuasive in transforming the policy discussion from 'what works' to 'what's feasible'.

We added agency officials as users for this study in Table 4.2. This is to reflect the fact that the expert views we put forward may have influenced senior officials in the Department of Education who had been regularly citing research as justification for their bilingual education policy position. After our report came out and we testified to Congress on the results, the Secretary gave no more speeches with the extreme interpretations of research evidence he had cited earlier.

With respect to the third study we presented, on tuition guarantees, we made no specific recommendations for action in our report and the congressional debate on the nature of future governmental higher education assistance will only start after this chapter is written. The programs we studied, however, are very different than the familiar tuition aid grants (and loans) now put forward as the principal government method of assisting students. It remains to be seen whether it would be feasible to try something like these private efforts as public ventures, and in times of tight funds whether the existing grant and loan programs could be squeezed slightly to permit further experiment with promising, but very different, alternatives. Despite the evidence of promise from our evaluation, those who benefit from the present arrangements might well resist such moves, even in the name of long-term improvement in access to higher education for the disadvantaged. Data alone will not solve this puzzle.

The second major observation is how hard it is to find the positive, and thus how hard it is sometimes to feel that evaluation is contributing to keeping hope alive. Several elements combine to lengthen the odds in the evaluator's search for good news:

- the growth of the poor, minority population of inner-city children who bring to school the hardest educational challenges;
- the continued deterioration of the environment beyond the school in many urban areas which sets cruel limits on the effectiveness of educators' best efforts;
- the diversity of educational practice which makes it hard to know what is happening and hard to find many comparable cases for analysis; and
- the diversity of goals for schooling and education in the United States, which makes for endless argument over what news counts as good.

We have deliberately shifted our approach, as shown in the third study reported above on tuition guarantees as motivators for school completion, to begin some evaluations we would not have done under the more typical criteria. (Those familiar criteria of evaluability would include such things as whether a significant program effort had been in place long enough and adequate data are available to warrant a study of effects.) In these new studies, we try to develop a model of what *can* work, drawing on past evaluations and theory. We act much as program designers would at this stage. We then search for programs which have the necessary elements, observe how they work, inspect outcome data that may be available to see if results match the predictions, and reach circumscribed conclusions about the *potential* of one or more approaches to the problem. The private sector tuition and mentoring programs, at least some of them, we found do have useful lessons in their design and implementation even though they are not widespread or not all effective. We also may be useful to designers by signalling those that seem especially unlikely to foster success in future. Since many honest evaluations in education must report bleak findings about programs offering small hope for improvement in results for young people, we were most pleased to be able to report on these promising private efforts, going well beyond the traditional scholarship grants of funds and offering intense and apparently effective help to disadvantaged youth.

We used a similar approach of building a model, based on past public health education as well as on the best knowledge of the new epidemic, and seeking strong examples of the model in practice, to suggest guidelines for AIDS education programs.[16] We are doing an evaluation of new methods of drug education this year in the same way.

## Resources for Inquiry in Education in the US

The Congress is keenly interested in the relevance, timeliness and technical adequacy of evaluations and other policy-making information produced by the executive branch departments. Indeed, we are also, for our own workload increases directly in proportion to the unreliability of basic data and evaluations from the departments; it is far preferable if we can review the performance of major systems and activities and not have to conduct basic program evaluations ourselves because others are not doing so adequately. For a key legislative committee we reviewed three types of education information produced or sponsored by the federal government: research, statistics and evaluations.[17]

We found problems in all three. Research activities shifted away from sponsorship of new studies to service-oriented activities such as dissemination, so much so that availability of up-to-date information to disseminate to teachers and other practitioners may be threatened. The new data-collection research that was done during the period we studied increasingly became narrowly focused and the scope of investigation was also restricted by abandonment of field-initiated work in favor of work increasingly prescribed by the federal sponsors. We found the quality of basic statistical information variable, with some problems that had persisted for decades. The major influence on information production was severe reductions in funding levels, with research funding down since the early 1970s by over 70 per cent in constant dollars (though the federal investment in education generally increased by 38 per cent in the same period). When the executive branch did request more money in recent years, congressional overseers of federal education research noted that they were unwilling to agree because of 'the highly politicized way in which funds were being handled' such as targeting scarce funds on conservative issues in education, including vouchers to help parents pay for private schools and concerns about 'immorality' in textbooks.

Though the department responded to our draft report saying that they were trying to restore some of the avenues for new data collection, which we commended, we had to note that at the time of our report in 1987 current levels of support for information activities remained dramatically lower than in 1980.

The good news is that education research and statistics funding did finally jump sizably in recent years, from $67 million in 1988 to $78 million in 1989 and reaching $96 million in 1990. The Commissioner of Education Statistics believes this is due in large part to our earlier stark analyses of the dwindling funds for education inquiry, our testimony on the subject (which received coverage in the newspapers as well as the education press), and due also to some renewed confidence in the executive branch as personnel changed following the presidential election in 1988.

### Conclusion

The GAO works at a long distance from the daily scenes of teaching and learning; we can hardly hope or try for the same influence as other nearer sources of analysis and advice. Our work aims to help the United States Congress ensure that its limited and targeted federal interventions are initiated on the soundest grounds possible and sustained only when effective.

In a complex policy environment, then, we have tried in GAO to contribute several kinds of evaluation to assist the national level of government — Congress and the executive branch — in the sorts of educational policy-making done there. We can point to some accomplishments, such as increases in support for inquiry, fewer weak claims about bilingual education, and perhaps greater realism about the limited prospects for certain regulatory kinds of educational reforms. As Congress works on higher education matters, we hope to see results from our report that intensive personal and financial efforts by committed sponsors can break a pattern of educational failure for disadvantaged youngsters.

## Notes

1 This chapter is a revised version of a paper presented at a conference on Educational Research and Evaluation for Policy and Practice, held at University of Warwick, September 1989. The views and opinions expressed by the authors are their own and should not be interpreted to be the policies or opinions of the US General Accounting Office.
2 Data on US education are drawn from annual volumes published by the US National Center for Education Statistics including *The Condition of Education*, which reports on selected indicators, and *Digest of Education Statistics*, which is comprehensive. Recent trends affecting education are powerfully summarized in Harold L. Hodgkinson (1985) *All One System: Demographics of Education, Kindergarten Through Graduate School*, Washington, DC, Institute for Educational Leadership.
3 National Commission on Excellence in Education (1983) *A Nation at Risk: The Imperative for Educational Reform*, Washington, DC, US Government Printing Office.
4 We reported in detail on this decline, based on a government-wide survey we do periodically, in US General Accounting Office (1987) *Federal Evaluation: Fewer Units, Reduced Resources, Different Studies From 1980* GAO/PEMD-87-9, Washington, DC, January. We also called attention to the 'erosion of evaluation capability' in a special report for Bush's then-incoming administration, *Program Evaluation Issues* (1988) GAO/OGC-89-8TR, Washington, DC, November.
5 On trends in student achievement generally and the effects of various factors in explaining them, including pre-school education, see *Educational Achievement: Explanations and Implications of Recent Trends* (1987) Washington, DC, Congressional Budget Office.
6 Allan Bloom (1987) *The Closing of the American Mind: Education and the Crisis of Reason*, New York, Simon and Schuster; E.D. Hirsch, Jr. (1987) *Cultural Literacy: What Every American Needs to Know*, New York, Houghton Mifflin.
7 One example of analysis of the situation and suggestions for change can be found in the report of the Task Force on Teaching as a Profession, *A Nation Prepared: Teachers for the 21st Century*, Washington, DC, Carnegie Forum on Education and the Economy, 1986.
8 National Center for Education Statistics (1990) *The Condition of Education 1990*, Vol. 2, *Postsecondary Education*, Washington, DC, US Government Printing Office.

9  The framework of purposes, users and types of study is outlined fully in Eleanor Chelimsky (1987) 'Linking Program Evaluation to User Needs', in Dennis J. Palumbo (Ed.) *The Politics of Program Evaluation*, Sage Yearbook in Politics and Public Policy, Beverley Hills, CA, Sage Publications.

10  For the full report of this study, see US General Accounting Office (1989) *Education Reform: Initial Effects in Four School Districts*, GAO/PEMD-89-28, Washington, DC, September. Requests for this and other GAO reports cited below may be sent to Box 6015, Gaithersburg, MD 20877, USA.

11  The full report is US General Accounting Office (1987) *Bilingual Education: A New Look at the Research Evidence*, GAO/PEMD-87-12BR, Washington, DC, March.

12  US General Accounting Office (1990) *Promising Practice: Private Programs Guaranteeing Student Aid for Higher Education*, GAO/PEMD-90-16, Washington, DC, June.

13  On the general subject, see Eleanor Chelimsky (1986) 'What Have We Learned About the Politics of Program Evaluation', address to the American Evaluation Association, October.

14  Our work examined only early effects in the selected cities, with data on only the first cohort of students who went through three years of secondary school and graduated under tougher standards. We acknowledged at the time that educators could refine their efforts in later years (our last data were from 1986) and that we thus underestimated the potential of this reform approach. However, accumulated nationwide testing results from the National Assessment of Educational Progress (NAEP) suggest that neither this reform strategy that we examined, nor others, have in combination produced much improvement in student outcomes. See Ina Mullis *et al.* (1990) *America's Challenge: Accelerating Academic Achievement. A Summary of Findings From 20 Years of NAEP*, Report 19-OV-01, Princeton, NJ, Educational Testing Service.

15  For details of how Congress used the GAO work in legislative action on bilingual education in 1987–88, see Eleanor Chelimsky and Frederick Mulhauser (1990) 'Helping Congress Sort Out Conflicting Claims About the Research Evidence on Bilingual Education', in *Readings on Equal Education, Vol. 10: Critical Issues for A New Administration and Congress*, New York, AMS Press.

16  US General Accounting Office (1988) *AIDS Education: Reaching Populations at Higher Risk*, GAO/PEMD-88-35, Washington, DC, September.

17  US General Accounting Office (1987) *Education Information: Changes in Funds and Priorities Have Affected Production and Quality*, GAO/PEMD-88-4, Washington, DC, November.

## Reference

COLEMAN, J.S. *et al.* (1986) *Equality of Educational Opportunity*, Washington DC, US Department of Health, Education and Welfare.

# 5    Voices of the Researched in a Report for Policy-Makers

*Colin Biott*

This chapter explores a number of questions raised by an attempt to represent the voices of the researched as well as the researcher in a final evaluation report which was addressed to policy-makers. It describes and discusses the use of three voices which differed according to whether they were individual or collective and the extent to which they were anonymous or identifiable. The report was of a two and a half-year study of an ESG Urban Primary School Project in three schools in a northern LEA from 1985 to 1988. As the evaluator, my main task was to provide evidence and maintain formative dialogue with the participants. The main forum for discussion was the steering group: the project team, the three headteachers, the LEA adviser, a teachers' union representative and an educational psychologist. I prepared interim reports to inform the decisions which shaped the project's progress and then at the end I wrote the final report for the Chief Officer.

It was important to me and to the steering group members that the final report would be consistent with the processes of the evaluation study in both form and meaning. In terms of meaning, we wished to convey the sense of community which we had tried to create between the participants and also between the reseacher and the researched. We also wanted to show our unfolding understanding of the uncertain and complex as well as the more straightforward aspects of our attempt to influence and improve practices in the schools. In choosing a form for the report, I had to take into account the audience and its relationship to the researched. During the evaluation we had tried to suspend notions of status and hierarchy, but we knew that the final report would be addressed to the Chief Officer. However much we told ourselves that this was an encouraging and supportive audience, we also felt the kind of vulnerability which arises from the anticipation of being judged. We needed an appropriate form for a public account of an unfinished, collaborative learning process which had been stopped at a predetermined point, but which would be read to discover the lessons that had been learnt.

On some issues, we were aware of the diversity of our individual voices, though on some others we could probably speak collectively. We thought, therefore, that it would be wrong for the report to have a simple message delivered in the single, impartial voice of the reseacher. It seemed necessary to give the report a plural rather than a unified structure — what Winter (1989) has called 'more of a collage than a description'. At the same time, it seemed rather limited and limiting to see the report as a mere collection of different viewpoints offered separately without interpretation.

The concept of voice has been useful in discussing the issues involved in report writing. It helps to draw attention to the meaning of what was spoken in the report, by whom it was spoken, in what form it was said and who was expected to be listening. It also hints at the importance of the earlier conversations between the participants as they negotiated the meaning of their personal and collective experiences in the project. Elbaz (1991) has emphasized recently the value of story as a form for making teachers' voices public, and in doing so she has used the image of 'a community of listeners':

> The sense of community of teachers and researchers, working together, listening to one another, is especially important at a time when the work of both groups is being increasingly bureaucratized (p. 16).

We had tried, both during the project and in the final report, to avoid assuming that some voices would be more credible than others. As Winter (1989) has said about the meaning of collaboration in research:

> everyone's point of view will be taken as a contribution to resources for understanding: no one's point of view will be taken as the final understanding as to what all the other points of view really mean (p. 56).

However, as Grumet (1990) has argued, this may be more difficult than it sounds. She has drawn attention to the politics of voice with particular reference to the voices of women, noting for instance, how the voice-over narrative on films is usually male and how 'the female voice is located in the interior of the film, often lodged in its recesses'

(p. 279). In the same way, I recognized the possibility that my own 'voice-over', could be so dominant that the voices of the researched would be hidden and unheard in the recesses of the report.

## The Types of Voices in the Report

The final report had four different voices. One of these was the researcher's voice: a summarizing voice speaking directly to the policy-makers, answering the questions they had asked at a late stage in the project. It was intended that this voice would represent the interests of those with most at stake over what would happen after the project came to an end. The recommendations made were those of the head-teachers and the staff of the three schools. For this reason, all statements which I wrote with what Grumet (1990) has called a voice of interpretation — the reflexive more distant, exterior voice-over — were carefully checked and redrafted. I shall return to the issue of speaking for others later in the chapter, but first I shall discuss the other three kinds of voices which are heard in the report:

1 The anonymous, authentic, individual voices speaking directly without interpretation: the teachers;
2 The identifiable, individual voices represented, without interpretation, through the researcher: the headteachers, the project team and the schools' curriculum leaders;
3 The collective voice spoken through the researcher, involving selection, interpretation and synthesis: the steering group.

There are, then, two important dimensions being used to describe the voices in the report: anonymity/identifiability and individuality/collectivity (shown in Figure 5.1). The use of these three types of voices shown in Figure 5.1 will be described, illustrated and discussed separately and then some general issues will be raised about the form and meaning of voice in evaluation reports.

## The Individual/Anonymous Voice

During the project I collected the kinds of evidence which would open up discussion about the concerns of the most vulnerable participants. There were times when it was the headteachers who were feeling most vulnerable. For example, at a time when it seemed that they should

Figure 5.1: Voices in the Report

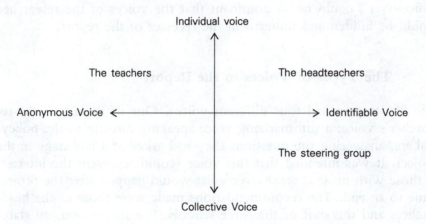

take the blame if their schools did not make good use of the project, one of them said that, 'this project is turning into self-evaluation for headteachers'. There was also a time when the project team was feeling bruised as a result of the indifference and resentment of the host teachers. At another time, my task was clearly to represent the views of the teachers who were generally unhappy about the imposition of an unwelcome project in their schools. It was as though someone was trying to put them back in Startrite shoes after they had learned to stand on their own, fully-formed feet.

My choice of methods to collect the views of the vulnerable, and to present them, varied at different times and for different participants. When I was first invited to work on the project it was for one specific and bounded job only. I was asked to collect the views of the teachers and to prepare a report for the steering group. This was one term after the start of the project and there was a great deal of open hostility towards it. At that time I knew nothing of the background which was causing this and I prepared a draft proposal, in which I suggested that I would interview the teachers. This was unacceptable to them. They said 'it smacked of appraisal', and by now a teachers' union had become involved. I met the teachers in their schools during assembly periods and following discussions about the project and the nature of my task, it was agreed that I should prepare a questionnaire on the points they had raised with me. The draft questionnaire was left in the schools for a week to check that it was acceptable, and subsequently all teachers completed it anonymously. I produced separate summaries for each school, and a composite summary for the steering group.

The teachers felt able to say what they wanted to say only if they

were protected by anonymity, and some of the anonymous statements they made at that time were subsequently included, with
their agreement, within the 'history' section of the final report. For
example:

> We were not consulted about our participation in the project
> and not sufficiently informed about our role over the next three
> years.

> If it failed, the present teachers would be expected to pick up
> the pieces. If it was successful, how could the staff be expected
> to maintain the activities which have required extra finance and
> staff?

It was not possible to guarantee complete anonymity in the interim reports which were written for insiders. Some people offered
comments for the report which they had already made frequently to
their colleagues in their staffrooms. In some cases, the vocabulary or
the structure of what was said was as recognizable as faces. What was
being being held back in the final report, however, was the kind of
background information which would render the teachers vulnerable
to identification by 'people in the office'. For this reason, we cannot
tell whether the persons making the comments were male or female,
or in early, mid or late career. We are not able to identify the school,
age range of children taught, any special subject interests or other sources
of current satisfactions and dissatisfactions in the job. To this extent
the teachers' anonymous voices lack the personal and professional dimensions which would give them life.

Although it did not redress this weakness completely, the teachers' comments in the final report are given focus and context. They
were invited to write comments on 'the history of the project' which
had already been agreed by the steering group as a fair summary of
what had happened. The teachers' comments were then added without
any editorial gloss, and 'the history' was left unchanged. They were
given the last word. Where they disagreed with the tone or content of
the account their voices remain a challenge to the 'official voice', and
as Grumet (1990) has said: 'the metaphor of voice has been most
persuasive when it has been used to challenge another speaker, thus
discriminating that speaker from another' (p. 278).

I have referred to the teachers' voices as plural and separate. They
wrote their comments privately and no attempt was made to summar-
ize or synthesize them into a single collective voice, a point to which

I shall return later. Their comments were printed unchanged in direct speech, as these examples show:

> It cannot be over-emphasized that the false start of the project was very much down to the way it was poorly structured, poorly presented and then inadequately represented to the teaching staff who were going to be such an intimate part of it.

> I did feel that the teaching staff came out of it [the summary] very badly. Some of us were less than enthusiastic because we were not consulted but informed that it had been decided that we would be involved.

> As usual the hard-working class teachers were not consulted. From the tone of [the summary] there is an implication that if the project is unsuccessful in its aims — the teachers are in the main to blame. However, if successful it is in spite of the teachers and great credit is due to the project team.

> The project members found it very rewarding with a small group, but were either unwilling or unable to demonstrate how it could be integrated into a class of about twenty-seven children.

> The impact was partial and incomplete e.g. some staff are still resentful that only a single year group should benefit.

> The team members were able to purchase apparatus/equipment which our school could not afford!!!

> There continued to be, throughout the project, distance between the staff and the 'team'. The label 'the team' did not help in any way in getting staff and the team members to work together.

> Despite the false start, I feel that there has been a much better take up than is made clear in the document. Even though there were fears of hidden agendas and at some stages an obvious lack of agenda, a wide cross-section of staff have proved themselves willing to participate, extend, or at the very least, explore some of the concepts brought up by the project members.

The overall impression of the document was that the majority of teachers were uncooperative and obstructive in their response to the project. . . . However once the project team were in school I feel that the majority of teachers gave their support to the team.

It is interesting to note that the people who have worked most closely with the members of the project team were not at the school when the project was introduced. These members of staff all work together and this has added to the them/us situation.

I find it noteworthy that the members of staff who have been most willing to 'open their doors' and be involved with the project were those teachers who joined the staff at the same time as the project team. They had escaped the negative feelings inspired by the poor way in which the project had been introduced to the staff.

The aims of the project were not fully discussed or explained to the teachers who joined the school after the start of the project. Unless you were personally involved with working with a team member you often did not know fully what was happening.

Communication would have been easier and a feeling of partnership stronger if the staff had been represented at steering committee meetings by a class teacher as well as by a head-teacher.

As a whole the school staffs have been unaware of changing aims and directions concerned within the project.

I felt I had only a vague idea about what the project hoped to achieve, and found it difficult to find out more. The summary illustrates throughout the lack of clear aims and the lack of communication between team members and the staff . . . lack of involvement in planning . . . concern about steering group minutes . . . a constant lack of communication.

The problem now seems to have swung from suspicion of 'what was it in aid of to one of, now we've taken it on board, 'will it all be in vain'! The staff will most definitely maintain the experience and added potential because of the project, but the children involved, the social situation of the school and the inherent problems remain untouched to a large extent. With the withdrawal of extra staffing and the majority of resources, the ability to do 'the extra something special' will almost certainly be lost.

After the project the LEA could help the schools concerned by helping to bring down the pupil/teacher ratio. In an EPA school, where the stress of a large class of 'disadvantaged' children can affect the health of a dedicated teacher, both teacher and pupils would benefit from a lower pupil–teacher ratio.

## The Individual/Identifiable Voice

Examples of individual, identifiable, voices are those of the three head-teachers. Since they were so few, and since it was not possible to avoid identifiable personal and professional contexts, their voices, like those of the project team and the school's curriculum leaders, could not be anonymous in the report. For this reason, we decided that their comments on the project would be written by me in reported speech. I interviewed them and prepared drafts which they edited.

The following example shows the kind of ideas which one head-teacher felt would sound better reported by me than they would being spoken directly by him using the personal pronoun 'I':

The headteacher of School A was the only one to have been in post from the beginning to the end of the project. He is an experienced headteacher who has seen many changes during his career. In his first headship he had a full-time teaching role, and administration had been so minimal that there was no need for a school clerk. Even in the early days of his present post, in a larger urban school, he had been able to maintain a 75 per cent teaching timetable. More recently he has seen a massive in-crease in paperwork needed to respond to administrators and the growing advisory service. In addition, there are more social problems to deal with and more crises requiring immediate attention. There have also been changes, such as more time being spent talking to parents, which are seen as worthwhile and positive, even though they take up more time. The unwelcome result of these changes has been a reduction in the amount of time which can be spent in classrooms. The project had increased his workload even further. There had been more meetings, more INSET and more clerical work had been necessary in order to keep people informed and to keep records of what had taken place. A major advantage, however, was that there was someone to work alongside teachers in their classrooms, 'to do what a good headteacher could have done in the past'.

As well as each speaking separately 'for themselves' the headteachers also wanted to have some things said for all three of them. The latter was presented in a section headed 'ideas held in common', which preceded their individual views and which was written in the same form. They felt that they could give more force to these statements by making them jointly. In the main, the comments they wanted to make were supportive of the teachers in the schools, while still acknowledging the overall value of the project and the commitment of the project team.

*Ideas held in common*

1   The day-by-day demands of teaching in urban primary schools can be emotionally draining and 'strength-sapping'. To say that the extra staffing from the project has been beneficial to the schools, was not to underestimate the extra work it gave to some members of the school staff.

2   The project teachers have shown a high level of commitment, perseverence, patience and integrity. The value of their contributions did not rest on them having special expertise which was normally absent in the schools. Indeed it was felt that some members of their own school staff could have fulfilled the project member role at the outset. What was valued was the project teachers' resilience, positiveness, willingness to share, listen, adapt and build relationships with a wide range of teachers.

3   The headteachers in post at the end of the project had all felt to some extent responsible for the professional development of the project teachers. It was generally thought that project team members had learned from working with some of the school staff, just as some of the teachers in the schools had learned from their involvement in the project.

4  The main value of the project has been in accelerating developments which would have been much slower, and which could probably not have been attempted concurrently. All heads could point to lasting benefits.

5  There is not enough known about the stresses and problems of running a difficult urban primary school. All recommend that a study of the role of the headteachers, working in these circumstances, is urgently needed.

## The Collective/Identifiable Voice

During the project, the steering group met monthly to review progress and to plan further developments. I became a member of this group after the first two terms when I had accepted the task of evaluator for the remainder of the project. My main tasks were, at different times, to provide evidence to elucidate issues and to raise issues or present ideas for discussion. Overall, I was expected to inform the processes of decision-making, and to keep a record of the development of the project. With regard to the latter task, it had been agreed at the outset that I should write a critical history of the project. I was, in a sense, the official chronicler. I was to tell the story of the project to a specific audience from the viewpoint of the steering group. That was a different job from the one in which I am now engaged as I write this chapter for an imaginary audience. The Czech novelist, Milan Kundera, has caught the nature of the difference:

> A woman who writes her lover four letters a day is not a graphomaniac, she is simply a woman in love. But my friend who xeroxes his love letters so he can publish them someday — my friend is a graphomaniac. Graphomania is not a desire to write letters, diaries, or family chronicles (to write for oneself or one's immediate family), it is a desire to write books (to have a public of unknown readers) (Kundera, 1983, pp. 91–92).

Kundera's warning about the graphomaniac's tendency to stop listening to other voices could also be appropriately aimed at evaluators:

> The invention of the printing press originally promoted mutual understanding. In the era of graphomania the writing of books has the opposite effect: everyone surrounds himself with his

own writings as with a wall of mirrors cutting off all voices from without (p. 92).

The writing of a 'public story' is a different task from retelling private and collective memories. When we recounted incidents we had shared, our understanding of the connections between them was taken for granted, but for the sake of coherence the public story would need clear themes or at least a series of connected phases. While we recognized this, we also thought that 'our' story should represent all perspectives without being oversimplified or distorted by contrived phases or themes.

Returning to Kundera's cautionary observations about the differences between writing for private and public audiences, it was important that the preparation of the public account should involve a conscious attempt to listen to other voices rather than to cut them off. This process of listening occurred in a number of stages. First, an unfolding series of drafts was read, checked and discussed by the steering group. Second, as referred to earlier, the final draft was read by the teachers and their comments were added, and third, the report was sent to the Chief Officer for clearance before it was sent from the LEA to the DES.

One factor which helped me in the task of writing with a 'collective voice' was the way that the story became shared as it grew. This was most apparent when we formed collective metaphors which caught the spirit of the project at a particular time. An example of this was the metaphor 'running with buckets'. This arose early in the project when one of the headteachers was consoling the team of support teachers which had become disheartened because of the way it was being marginalized by the host teachers. 'Don't worry', he said, 'you can take a horse to water but you can't make it drink.' Others joined in the conversation: 'Yes, but in this case the water is being taken to the horses!' After we had conjured up a number of amusing images, we made an enduring imaginary picture of the support teachers running along corridors leaving buckets brimming with water at each classroom door, and returning in the hope that they would see signs of one of the teachers having taken a sip.

In this way we soon began to build a history of shared experiences and ways of talking about them which gave us a sense of belonging. We had constructed, retrospectively, a number of almost discrete phases which we could look back to as symbols of the pain that we had overcome in the project's history. It was rather like a family looking at an album of old photographs and saying how much younger they all look now. When I came to identify the project's phases and to give them subtitles, I found that I had most of them already in my fieldnotes. Taken together, the subtitles themselves suggest a theme of development from the imposition of an unwelcome project to a partnership between the schools and the support team in which the host teachers take the lead and then begin to demand further support for their schools:

1 Being Targeted: suspicion, defence and hostility,
2 Attempting to Overcome Bad Beginnings: 'Running with Buckets',
3 Consultation and Participation in Planning and Review,
4 Collegiality and the Project Team as Learners,
5 A Form of Self-Evaluation for Heads,
6 Curriculum Leaders as Project Leaders: Project Members as Support Teachers,
7 Tensions: Vestiges of Resistance v. Increased Project Momentum,
8 Evidence of Impact and a Plea for Continued Support from the LEA after the Project,
9 A Blur between Project and School Initiatives,
10 What has the LEA Learned?

Because it is positive and optimistic, the story of the project offers a form in which to discuss, constructively, the weaknesses and problems we encountered. It also shows the questions that we asked ourselves. It places them in context and locates them without attaching lasting blame.

The following extracts refer to the period from January to June 1987 (phases 4–7 above). This was a time when some of the early difficulties had been overcome and the schools were beginning to take control of the pace and direction of the project. The amount of staff discussion was said to be increasing at that time, and the focus was shifting to the whole staff working together rather than to individuals being offered separate support. Much was being made of the ways that the project team members were learning from the host teachers.

Woven into the story, however, are references to vestiges of deep resentment and to some difficult incidents which convey the feelings of unease which still remained. Although the history was told with the collective voice of the group which was responsible for steering the project, there was a conscious attempt to avoid a self-congratulatory management report. The fact that I knew that the participating teachers would be the first readers helped to stop that happening.

*January/February 1987: Collegiality and Project Team as Learners*

In the early part of the term the attention of the steering group moved to 'the collegial approach to change'. This was described as a 'tolerable modification' rather than redefinition of project aims. Heads listed and described the types of work going on in their schools (e.g. visits, parental involvement, learning with computers) and reporting on the positive reactions to the 'Stress INSET'. At the same time much significance was being given to the way in which the project was 'affecting the amount and intensity of staff discussion'. Could the project lead to the valuing of learning through discussing? Would it affect teachers' views of their role and would it lead to a 'continuity of philosophy' across the schools, especially in the 'un-owned areas' like corridors?

As these kinds of questions were being addressed, a number of others were being raised:

As the involvement of staff becomes wider will the resistance of the few become more hardened?

What ways are there to facilitate any change of stance of those who have previously set themselves explicitly and assertively against the project?

Does the focus on a 'collective approach to change', constitute a challenge to the existing school cultures?

These questions shifted the emphasis into areas in which the project team could have little direct influence, in that it could not effectively coordinate corporate developments within the schools. Its indirect influence in enhancing collegiality was in giving individual teachers an experience of collaborative planning, teaching and evaluation. This idea was to be elaborated at a later stage.

During the February meeting, the team members indicated that they themselves were learning a great deal through collaborating and talking with teachers in the schools. In successful partnerships they felt like colleagues. They were still seeking to relinquish the 'expert' label which the early history of the project had imposed on them. Perhaps it was still being used, however, by those who were continuing to distance themselves from the project. The wording of the original advertisement for the jobs was still being cited to justify the resentment.

*March 1987: A Form of Self-Evaluation for Heads?*

The March meeting of the steering group followed an HMI visit. A further whole-day meeting of the group was also held at the end of the month. Its purpose was to plan further developments. The new project coordinator was able to attend prior to taking up her post after the vacation.

At the first meeting, a number of guiding principles were decided after discussion of the HMI feedback and after the group's own reflections in light of this:

1 Where possible, time should be set aside for planning and review when individuals or groups of teachers work with the project;
2 The project should avoid the decontextualized provision of resources;
3 There should be a concentration of focus in the project;
4 There should be an increase in emphasis on understanding children's learning;
5 Participants should be considering the long-term benefits to the schools, so that there is some continuity after the project.

This discussion was, in effect, confirming and strengthening the view that it was not enough for some individual teachers to have benefited. The whole school should be corporately affected. At the beginning of the whole-day planning meeting, the group explored the implications of this idea. As one headteacher said, 'the project is becoming a form of self-evaluation for heads'.

The current position was that there were 'pockets of teamwork' in which the project team members were finding effective roles. In addition many other teachers were affected informally and indirectly. It was acknowledged that the team would not be expected to try to achieve a working relationship with every teacher in the schools.

There was some discussion by the headteachers about the extent to which they might attempt to influence the pattern of involvement at this stage. The whole steering group was to benefit from this time onwards, as headteachers began to share their collective understanding of the nature of this complex task. The significance of the steering group as a learning forum for its members should not be underestimated. Its reflections about processes of professional development and school improvement were characteristic of a shifting emphasis in aspiration for the whole project.

Following the HMI visit, the group began to think about the possibility of there being 'weak' and 'strong' aspects of the project. The strong aspect was where teachers and team members were sharing the planning, teaching and reviewing of learning. They would be thinking aloud together about children's learning experiences, and also learning themselves through joint experience and dialogue. They would be able to conceptualize their long-term professional development needs. The weaker side of the project would be characterized by an exclusive and pragmatic emphasis on immediate resource needs, 'cover' or, 'an extra pair of hands'.

*Curriculum Leaders as Project Leaders, Project Members as Support Teachers*

So far, the project could be said to have been grafted onto the formal organization of leadership and support in the schools. If it was to become embedded in these formal practices, and if the headteachers were to take responsibility for the development of the project, then it would need to be integrated into the framework through which the headteachers were currently working. At this stage, the curriculum leaders in the schools would become 'the project leaders' for their schools. They would take responsibility, in conjunction with the headteachers, for the planning, coordination and review of a project of the schools' choice.

From about this time there were some subtle, but significant, shifts in the terminology which was being used. Perhaps because of the leadership for projects moving explicitly to the schools, and perhaps because of the new ESG Project

Coordinator's previous experience of leading another LEA support team (in special educational needs), the members were referred to as 'support teachers' by some of the participants. Section 6 of this report refers to the way in which some of the school staff and team-members saw the relationship between their roles. Labels were seen as important, as one of the curriculum leaders said, 'I don't call them "the team". I call them by their names — by their first names.'

The following principles were agreed at this stage:

1  Teachers should have the opportunity to work with another teacher in their own classrooms. It was agreed that 'shared planning, teaching and reflecting is the central aim'. Colleagues on the school staff could be partners (not just the project team). The talk between the partners should be mainly about the children's learning (rather than classroom organization);

2  The school staff should be involved in project planning;

3  Planning and evaluating time should be made available, and recognized as important, for discussions between teachers, between teachers and 'the team', between teachers and the headteachers, and within the team itself;

4  Processes of dissemination and liaison between the schools should help to give the project its coherence, during a period in which the separate schools might have different needs for support;

5  Thought should be given to forming a base for continuity and development within the schools after the end of this project. People with leadership responsibilities should develop their approaches to working with colleagues through being given some additional time, support and opportunity for sharing reflections. Staff should become more convinced of the value of talking, thinking and learning together.

The headteachers of the schools had come to the meeting ready to indicate their own school's choice of focus. These were:

*School A*: For the team to help facilitate the implementation of policy in environmental studies and science, including mathematical and language development. The 'post-holders' for environmental studies and science would lead the work. Their discussion document had already been issued to staff at this point. The LEA adviser for environment studies had been consulted and he would be directly involved as required. The emphasis in the curriculum discussion document was on experiential learning and the development of skills. The intention would be to involve all classes in work on the same theme, thus facilitating discussion about progression in learning.

*School B*: For the team to help with the policy-making process. The staff had jointly identified science as the focus for the next term. A new 'post-holder' had been appointed and he had already begun to collect information about the kind of lessons being taught. The theme for the whole school would be 'colour'. It was intended that the work would be skills-based and that it could become cross-curricular. Other post-holders would also be involved in its development. The team would be asked to assist with the provision of 'organic resources' to support the actual teaching and learning taking place. During this period the 'post-holder' for science would be preparing the curriculum policy document and would be seeking support in that task.

*School C*: For one particular project member to work with a team of reception class teachers and the headteacher. The purpose would be to develop practice, particularly for the 4-year-old children. Guiding principles would be refined through shared teaching, observation and reflection. This would build on work already started to integrate play with other forms of learning, and to enhance the integral processes of identifying and recording children's learning. The intention would be to promote a similar practice in other year-groups through widening the discussion.

*May/June 1987: Tensions: Vestiges of Resistance v. Increased Project Momentum*

At the May and June meetings of the steering group there were discussions which, to some extent, served to remind the group of the suspicion and resentment which the establishment of the project had generated.

Headteachers reported, at the May meeting, that some staff had been concerned about the minutes of the previous steering group meeting. They wanted 'a clearer explanation of the change in project aims'. It was agreed that the minutes were an accurate record of the meeting, and that the problem was a signal to try to improve the communication between the steering group and the school staffs.

Perhaps the divide between the 'reflective' and 'pragmatic' dimensions of the project was being felt, now that the value of thinking and working together was being emphasized. The steering group, as a forum for reflection, was itself a cause of concern for some teachers. It was seen as essential but potentially divisive.

At the outset the steering group minutes had been confidential, but from November 1985 they were made available to all staff. Even so, it was felt that further steps could be taken to improve communication:

— Heads should have the agenda in suffcient time to discuss it with staff prior to the meeting,
— Those staff leading current initiatives could represent their schools on the steering group,
— A bulletin to which staff could contribute,
— An open meeting for all staff about the project,
— A paper to be drawn up to show redefined aims.

At the June meeting, there was some discussion of a problem which had grown from an interpretation of the HMI's suggestion that there should be time for the teachers and project members to plan and review together. In five cases in one school, the 'evaluations' had been written, shared and held as confidential by the partners. This had evidently caused some anxiety — 'enough to set the project right back'. It seemed that some of the concern had been expressed by teachers who were not directly involved.

One headteacher wished to know how many such reports had been written and who would read them. It was made clear that only the appropriate partners had seen them and that they would not be seen by any other person.

The headteacher's concern was first, that it was unacceptable that heads should not know what was going on in their schools, and second that they would be unable to give their support where it may be needed. After some discussion it was agreed that any future review of shared work would be verbal and not recorded in writing.

The way in which headteachers checked for any hidden agenda was an indication of their concern to 'reassure and protect' their staff. It also showed that there was still some uneasiness about the whole project. Previous events and incidents were still being recalled to illustrate the foundations of the suspicion. At this meeting, the group was reminded of an incident at a management course, shortly after the project was announced, when another head said to the head of one of the project schools, 'It's a stigma on the schools concerned . . . the head is no longer in charge'.

## Conclusion

Looking back, then, my researcher's voice has been dominant, and this has been justified partly as an attempt to speak for other individuals and groups. The form of the report with its different viewpoints does offer scope for readers to make reinterpretations of what happened, but overall I had control of the presentation of all of these different views. I am, therefore, open to accusations of placing my limitations on the quality of what is said and how it is said. I may be deluding myself in assuming that I am conveying a sense of plurality, while what I am actually doing is inadvertently getting in the way of direct communication between each voice and its listeners.

The most direct form of communication comes from the individual teachers, and the report would have been improved if it had also included a similarly direct, collective, teachers' voice. While this may have added force to what they said, it would have been difficult to organize and it would also have been hard to convey the internal contradictions which are apparent in the collection of individual statements. If a collective teachers' voice is sought in future evaluation studies, the writing would probably be best undertaken by one of the teachers themselves. This would mean building it into the design of the project as an integral part of its professional development dimension. One of the teachers could be given the time to act as an official chronicler of the learning experiences of colleagues. This would neither eliminate the problems of speaking for others, nor the pitfalls of the contrived consensus, but at least it would add a second voice-over to the final report.

There are plausible reasons for approaching the writing of a final evaluation report in the way we did it. First, the participants did not have the time and many lacked the inclination to write about a project which was ending. Second, there are risks involved in presenting our own individual views directly to those with influence over our professional futures. Third, the report was addressed to policy-makers whose expectations needed to be taken into account. They commissioned the study and their intention was to learn from it. They sought clear recommendations and a succinct summary of what was learnt.

What was being attempted, then, was a kind of compromise. We tried to place alternative and sometimes contradictory views and records of experience in one coherent report. This report could be read selectively for its recommendations, or in more detail for inherent tensions and contradictions between the viewpoints. The different voices presented included those of the steering group in the form of a story of the project's history, the headteachers, the curriculum leaders, and the project team in the form of identifiable, individual and collective comments, and the teachers in the form of anonymous, individual and direct reactions to the 'history of the project' section. The value of these different voices rests mainly on the extent to which they challenge each other and help to build our understanding of the multidimensional nature of an attempt to change teachers and schools.

## References

ELBAZ, F. (1991) 'Research on teacher's knowledge: The evolution of a discourse', *Journal of Curriculum Studies*, **23**, 1, pp. 1–19.

GRUMET, M.R. (1990) 'Voice: The search for a feminist rhetoric for educational studies', *Cambridge Journal of Education*, **20**, 3, pp. 277–82.

KUNDERA, M. (1983) *The Book of Laughter and Forgetting*, London, Penguin Books (first published in France in 1979).

WINTER, R. (1989) *Learning from Experience: Principles and Practice in Action Research*, London, Falmer Press.

# 6    Inspection, Time-Constrained Evaluation and the Production of Credible Educational Knowledge

*Brian Wilcox*

## Introduction

Increasing emphasis is being given to the importance of inspection as a major means of evaluating education and training provision. This can be seen in the success of Her Majesty's Inspectorate (HMI), since the mid-1970s, to re-establish an influential national role in which inspection was central (Lawton and Gordon, 1987). In the training field a new inspectorate, the Training Standards Advisory Service, was set up in 1986 to inspect the Youth Training Scheme. Most recently of all, local education authority (LEA) advisory services have been given an enhanced inspection function as a consequence of the Education Reform Act (1988).[1] The growth of inspectorates is also apparent beyond education, for example, in the social services (Day and Klein, 1990). In addition, the Audit Commission, established in 1983, has interpreted its remit to encompass a broad inspectorial role in the public services generally.

Despite these developments, inspection tends to be ill-understood both as a concept and a practice. The purpose of this chapter is to attempt to redress the situation by relating inspection to the concept of evaluation on the one hand, and to the creation of educational knowledge on the other. This constitutes part of the context for presenting the results of a national project on inspection methodology[2] which will be reported in full elsewhere (Wilcox, 1992).

## Evaluation, Monitoring and Inspection

One of the important consequences of the Education Reform Act in the Government's view is that LEAs should develop a more systematic approach to the evaluation of the services which they and their institutions provide. A key role is envisaged for local advisory services — increasingly being referred to as local inspectorates.

> The local inspectorates will need to monitor and evaluate school performance. They will need to provide LEAs and the schools themselves with trusted and informed professional advice, based on first-hand observation of what schools are actually doing. Doing all of these things well requires inspection in all its forms (Secretary of State, 1988, paras 10/11).

This activity will be particularly linked to the introduction of schemes of local management of schools which involve formula funding and the delegation of financial and managerial responsibilities to governing bodies.

> Local management of schools represents a major educational initiative which . . . LEAs . . . will need to evaluate. . . . LEAs should aim to generate as part of their monitoring cycle appropriate data with which to evaluate the success of their schemes. This evaluation should serve two purposes. First, LEAs will need to assess their success in implementing their schemes in the initial period. . . . Secondly, LEAs will need to evaluate on an ongoing basis the success of local management in improving the quality of teaching and learning in their schools (DES, 1988a, para. 155).

The development of the kind of monitoring and evaluation programme implied by the above will pose a formidable challenge to many LEAs. Up until recently at least, the evaluation function has generally been poorly developed in LEAs. While evaluation has nominally been a major responsibility of advisory services, few LEAs have seriously thought through the implications or provided a consistent and coherent programme of support to make it a reality. The consequences have been, as the most recent study appears to suggest (Stillman and Grant, 1989; Stillman, 1989), that evaluation is a minority activity in many advisory services and consists of such a bewildering array of apparently different approaches as to indicate considerable conceptual and methodological confusion.

Part of the problem lies in the lack of clarity which surrounds key concepts and procedures. In particular the meanings ascribed to monitoring, evaluation and inspection are often assumed to be self-evident and are often used synonymously. *Evaluation* as understood by educational evaluators, represents a notion which goes beyond the usual dictionary definitions (for example, 'ascertain amount of', 'find numerical expression for', 'appraise', 'assess'). For many evaluators an appropriate definition would be 'the systematic collection and interpretation of evidence leading, as part of the process, to a judgment of value with a view to action' (Wolf, 1987, p. 8). This definition succinctly incorporates four important attributes. First, that evaluation is based on evidence which is *systematically* collected. Second, that the meaning of evidence is seldom unambiguous and therefore needs to be *interpreted*. Third, that *judgments of value* are made not only about how well an educational institution or programme is meeting its goals but also the contribution being made to larger educational and social aims. Finally, evaluation is *action oriented*; it is intended to lead to better policies and practices.

The word *monitoring* is frequently used in conjunction with that of evaluation although it seems to lack an agreed definition. For example the term is not listed in the *British Educational Thesaurus* (Marder and Johnston, 1988). Monitoring is perhaps most familiar in non-educational contexts. For example, the progress towards building a house is monitored by site visits noting the stages of construction against previously agreed plans, schedules and specifications. The financial probity of an organization is monitored through the standard procedures of accounting and auditing. These examples suggest that the general process of monitoring involves the collection of information on a regular basis, in order to check on the progress of an activity or the state of a system, with the intention that significant departures from the expected lead to some appropriate corrective action.

The implication is that monitoring relies upon the identification of objective indicators which can be reliably assessed against predetermined standards or targets. The more indicators which are used, the greater will be the amount of available information about the entity being monitored. The information may be capable of an interpretation which is essentially evaluative or it may prompt additional activity and the collection of further information which makes a subsequent evaluation possible. In other words, monitoring is an ongoing process carried out on a system in order to yield regular information about aspects of its condition or level of functioning. Each bit of monitoring information is minimally evaluative in the sense that reaching (or exceeding) the target or standard is considered to be better than falling below it. The more the individual bits of monitoring information can be interpreted and aggregated to give a comprehensive description of the quality and effectiveness of the system, the more monitoring can be said to shade into evaluation.

Evaluations are often conceived of as discrete one-off exercises. Indeed much of the literature on evaluation derives from such exercises. While there is clearly a need for specific evaluations within an LEA, the linking of monitoring and evaluation implies that an ongoing process of evaluation, deriving from regular monitoring, will be a major means for assessing institutions and programmes.

*Inspection* is an example of a method of evaluation which is surprisingly poorly documented in the literature. There are probably several reasons for this neglect. Much of the writing on evaluation derives from the USA where inspection is not a feature of the public education system. Evaluation there has been largely conducted by external evaluators appointed to funded programmes. Another reason may relate to the fact that the main contributors to evaluation theory and methodology, including those in Great Britain, have been academics and educational researchers. They may not therefore have recognized the work of inspectors as falling within the legitimate parameters of evaluation as they understand them. A further reason is that the outcomes of inspection, in the form of HMI reports, have only within the last few years been publicly available and open to scrutiny by researchers and others (see Gray and Hannon, 1986). Inspection then has tended to be a somewhat shadowy and ill-understood approach to the monitoring and evaluation of the public education system. This is particularly regrettable since it is arguable that much of what is known about education in the public domain has been influenced more by the findings of HMI than by those of researchers and professional evaluators.

The distinction between evaluation, monitoring, and inspection can be illustrated by considering the likely response to the requirement that governing bodies should make an annual return outlining the curriculum provision in their schools (DES, 1989a).[3] The return provides a structured format for showing the organization of the total curriculum offered by a school and how the subjects of the National Curriculum are to be accommodated. The return is essentially a monitoring tool in which information (on the curriculum) is collected on a regular basis (annually), for subsequent scrutiny (inspection). Although no definite quantitative standards or targets are required (that is, a subject does not have to be taught in a particular timetabled way for a fixed number of periods per week), the return must make apparent the likelihood that the National Curriculum will be adequately covered by the curriculum organization favoured by the school. If this assurance seems in doubt then the LEA has the opportunity of following the matter up.

The information obtained from the curriculum return is, of itself, only weakly evaluative. Knowing that the school is adequately accommodating the structure of the National Curriculum does not necessarily say anything about the quality of the learning involved. This would require a special exercise in which the experience of pupils is examined at first hand. This could be done by staff within the school (self-evaluation) or by 'outsiders' (inspection).

In due course, schools and LEAs will have access to other monitoring information which bears on the issue of the quality of pupil learning. The assessment of pupils on standard assessment tasks (SATs) of the National Curriculum will provide quantitative expressions of the level of pupils' learning. However, SATs by themselves cannot provide a comprehensive and exhaustive account of learning outcomes. In other words, although SATs may sharpen the focus of evaluations (whether school self-evaluation or inspection) they will not make such evaluations redundant.

## Inspection, Judgment and Credible Knowledge

Most of us are able, when required, to comment on an educational institution or programme with which we are familiar. For example, when asked about a particular school, the response might be something like 'X is a good school, the pupils are well-behaved, it gets good exam results, and many pupils go on to higher education'. Such a response is both descriptive and evaluative and is often made off the top of the head. These kinds of instantaneous evaluations are the stuff of daily life whether one is a teacher in a classroom, an administrator or inspector, an academic educationist, or indeed a parent. Despite their ubiquity we know very little about how we come to make them or how they influence our subsequent actions. It seems that they are based on tacit norms which normally evade articulation and expression, (see Schon, 1983, pp. 49–69).

In contrast, judgments may be made on the basis of apparently more systematic approaches. *Systematic evaluation* in education is described in a substantial literature which has grown rapidly in the last few decades. Although the literature reveals considerable diversity in terms of the assumptions, methods and purposes of educational evaluation there are nevertheless some common features. Evaluation is conceived of as a form of investigation or enquiry, carried out by specialists empathetic to a research tradition, using specific techniques and methods and operating within a clear theoretical or conceptual framework. Some of the most influential contributions to the literature have emerged from evaluations carried out within a time-scale (frequently of several years' duration) characteristic of major research studies and often with substantial external funding allowing the appointment of full-time evaluators. Furthermore the focus of such evaluations have tended to be on individual projects and programmes of an innovative nature rather than on institutions and existing provision.

Evaluation may be usefully understood in terms of a continuum with systematic evaluation located at one end, and everyday judgment at the other. Somewhere within this spectrum is a band which represents intermediate approaches to evaluation. These seek to be more explicit, public and rigorous than everyday judgments while approximating where they can to the thoroughness of systematic evaluation.

The approaches I have especially in mind here are those adopted by inspectors and advisers. Advisers and inspectors are required to carry out evaluations as a regular part of their professional roles, although seldom are they their only task. The framework within which they tend to operate is one which is governed more by the categories and assumptions of professional practice rather than those derived from a research or theoretical background. The methods which they employ are closer to those of everyday life than the often specialist techniques used by evaluators. The outcomes of their evaluations (inspections) are addressed primarily to practitioners rather than the educational research community. As a result their reports are cast in a language and style more appropriate to the former than to the latter.

Unlike the majority of evaluators, inspectors tend to be concerned with a range of aspects of the education system as it is *typically* rather than with discrete and frequently innovative projects. Inspectors and advisers seldom have the comparative luxury of being able to concentrate most of their effort on a single evaluation conducted over a substantial period of time. More than other evaluators they are constrained by tight time-scales measured in days rather than months or years.

The conditions under which advisers and inspectors operate as evaluators are likely to be similar to those of other practitioners who are required from time to time to carry out evaluations as part of their normal duties. These will include teachers, senior staff of schools and colleges and education officers. There is no accepted term which describes the evaluation approaches of this diverse group of practitioners. Because it is the time dimension which perhaps most significantly distinguishes this group from full-time evaluators, I propose to refer to them provisionally as exponents of *time-constrained evaluation*. Inspection then is one example of time-constrained evaluation. It is one which has a long tradition (the history of HMI goes back to 1839), although surprisingly little is known about individual practice and methodology. It is necessary to understand the nature of inspection better than we do. This understanding is not only to inform the practice of those specifically designated as inspectors but also that of others who may be required to carry out time-constrained evaluation as part of their duties.

An alternative way of regarding time-constrained evaluators is as producers of knowledge of the education system. Ideally such knowledge needs to be generated on a regular basis allowing appropriate updating to reflect both the complexity and the dynamic nature of an education system. Moreover the knowledge must be credible both to practitioners and the public. *Practitioner-credible knowledge* is necessary for those responsible for the planning and development of the education service — whether at institutional, local or national levels. *Publicly credible knowledge* is necessary to foster a citizenry informed about educational matters. It is crucial for a society which aspires to be democratic to have reliable knowledge of its education system — and for that knowledge to be widely disseminated. Such knowledge is especially necessary at a period, like the present one, of radical change. This is not only because education makes heavy demands on the public purse but because it is a major influence on the development of individuals and society. People therefore need to know what the aims, methods and achievements of the educational system are in order to judge them critically and have a voice in their development.

The creation of practitioner and publicly credible knowledge is not a new responsibility of the education service. Although not traditionally expressed in these terms, it is a responsibility which has always been implicit in the very conception of a locally managed education service subject to democratic control. An education service, if it is to be rationally managed and made accountable, requires a credible knowledge base. The advent of the Education Reform Act makes such a base absolutely imperative. The delegation of many management responsibilities, formerly exercised by the LEA, to individual institutions is an inherently risky business. The Act therefore holds LEAs accountable for keeping track of how institutions manage themselves while, at the same time, observing national and local policies.

The consequences of the Act are also to increase 'consumer choice' in education and to foster competition between institutions operating within an educational 'market'. In other words, a credible and useful knowledge base is necessary on the one hand to those responsible for strategic planning and development within a devolved system, and on the other to the new educational consumers wishing to choose between potentially competing institutions. Although time-constrained evaluation will make a major contribution to an LEA-wide knowledge base — and it is the one which I am particularly concerned with here — it will not be the only one. For example, LEA and institution-based management information systems are already being installed to support the delegation of financial and management responsibilities. These will play a vital part in the greater availability of educational knowledge that the Act will require. Coordinating the creation and use of the knowledge base will be a major responsibility of LEAs under the new Act.

## Inspection and the Generation of Credible Educational Knowledge

It is important to be clear what the term 'inspection' implies. Educational inspection is concerned with the monitoring and evaluation of institutions, services, programmes and projects. It is carried out by one or more persons (inspectors) who are external to and independent of the entity being inspected. The aim is to gain first-hand knowledge of what is being inspected by observing it in operation and through direct encounter with those centrally involved. The outcome is usually a report to those responsible. In addition to providing a description and evaluation, a report will usually set out suggestions for further development. Perhaps for most people, the notion brings to mind the long established HMI practice of the 'full' inspection in which a team of inspectors will spend a week in a school or college looking at the range of its provision and activities.

Full inspection however is but one type among several determined by the various possible combinations of: the number of inspectors involved (from lone individuals to teams of twenty or more); the specialisms of the participating inspectors (whether subject, phase or a mix of the two); and the number and type of aspects being inspected (schools, colleges, departments, projects etc). Thus inspections can range from a day visit by a specialist inspector to a single department to multidisciplinary teams working for a week or so in a large school or college. In addition, the findings of individual inspections may be aggregated into studies of specific LEAs and even major aspects of national educational provision. It is probably this complete range of activities that is implied in the use of the phrase 'inspection in all its forms'.

A number of possible criteria may be identified for judging the credibility of educational knowledge. First there is the question of the *impartiality* of those who produce it. The impartiality of HMI is to a very large extent based on its independence. This independence is exemplified in three ways:

1 the Senior Chief Inspector (SCI) has direct access to the Secretary of State;
2 although the work of HMI reflect the priorities of the Secretary of State, HMI decides what to inspect, and how to inspect it, as the basis for advice provided;
3 HMI reports as it finds. Although the decision to publish or not lies with the Secretary of State, anything that is published must be as HMI wrote it.

Independence is not to be confused with organizational accountability. Thus while the SCI is accountable to the Permanent Secretary, s/he is able to present an inspectorate view on any matter to the Secretary of State. This may be especially important at times when new policies are being considered. Once a particular policy has been decided, HMI is required to work within its framework and cannot publicly oppose it. HMI however continues to have the professional independence of being able to report on the *consequences* of the policy. The right of being able to provide an HMI view directly, if necessary, to the Secretary of State is an extremely important one. It reflects the fact that the views of HMI are distinctively based upon experience informed by the direct and regular observation of the education service through the process of inspection. In an LEA it is the Chair of Education, the Chief Education Officer and the Chief Adviser (or Inspector) who can be regarded as analogous figures to the Secretary of State, the Permanent Secretary and the Senior Chief Inspector at national level. In the past however, in few LEAs have Chief Advisers had a level of independence comparable to that enjoyed by the SCI.

Another factor which helps to guarantee the independence of HMI, and thus the impartiality of its judgments, is that it is not involved directly in the management of the educational institutions and programmes which it inspects. HMI therefore has no personal or professional stake in them and is not beholden to those who are responsible for their management. The corresponding situation is not so clear for

LEA advisers. Although advisers are not responsible for the management of schools and colleges they may be very closely involved through their specialist or general support work. This may lead, as has sometimes been suggested, to advisers inspecting aspects of provision in which they themselves have been heavily implicated through advising, supporting and in some cases even managing. Questions of conflict of interest may therefore arise and could weaken the claim to impartiality. Anxieties of this kind presumably lie behind the following comment of a former Permanent Secretary:

> Can we be confident that inspection will not be constrained by blueprints of good practice or particular axes to grind? We expect local inspectors to report what in their professional judgment they find — just as HMI do (Hancock, 1988, p. 2).

An LEA therefore needs to be able to demonstrate that the evaluations which are made on its behalf (whether through inspection or in other ways) and the judgments that they enshrine are impartial, that is, not subject to the pressures of local political, administrative and institutional self-interest. This will require a clear indication of how evaluation relates organizationally to the other major functions of the LEA. Following the Education Reform Act, many LEAs have reorganized their existing departmental structures. Several different models are already apparent, including the establishment of inspectorates and new divisions of 'quality assurance'. How these new structures will work in practice remains to be seen. If however the public is to have confidence in the new LEAs, they will need to show that they are able to provide impartial information about the quality of their service.

Guaranteeing this impartiality will continue to be problematic. The question can always be asked, 'Can we, the public, be sure of the impartiality of those evaluating the educational provision of an LEA which is also their paymaster and employer?' A useful general principle is that impartiality is more likely to be observed the less closely the evaluator is professionally involved with the entity being evaluated. This would suggest that external evaluation (inspection) of an institution or programme is generally less open to the charge of partiality than one carried out by the staff within it (self-evaluation). A consequence of the principle might be that in some cases the adviser to a particular school would not be included in its evaluation or, at the very least, not given the main responsibility for carrying it out.

Impartiality, like any other virtue, is gained only by its continued conscious practice. HMI has won its claim to independence and therefore impartiality over many years. This has been maintained despite the increasing politicization of education nationally. The HMI ability to report without fear or  favour is nowhere better seen than in the series of annual reports of the SCI published since 1983 (e.g. DES, 1989b). These reports provide critical summaries of the effects of Government and LEA educational policies.

Confidence in inspectors' accounts of the education service is based upon beliefs about the appropriateness of their experience. This experience is of two types: general educational experience; and experience of monitoring and evaluation. Recognition of *educational experience* (and expertise) is probably the principal reason why teachers have confidence in what inspectors say and write. Given the professional aspirations of teachers it would generally be regarded as inappropriate for inspection to be carried out by those who had not themselves been successful experienced teachers. The demonstrable possession of these chacteristics is an essential requirement for appointment to HMI. The academic and other professional qualifications of HMI are also substantial. For example, in excess of 40 per cent of the current complement hold a higher degree — a proportion well in excess of that of the teaching force as a whole. Similar criteria apply to the appointment of LEA advisers who have an average level of qualification and prior seniority in school or college greater than that of the general teaching force (Stillman and Grant, 1989).

*Experience of monitoring and evaluation* has not perhaps in the past been seen as an essential feature of inspectorate credibility. This however is likely to change. There are several reasons why this kind of credibility will gain increasing prominence. First, there is the undeniable growth of educational evaluation as a specialist field over the last 20 or more years. This had had the effect of demonstrating that the processes of learning and educational development generally are complex and that the task of making judgments about them far outstrips the knowledge gained *simply* from having been a teacher — albeit a successful one. Second, ideas about the significance and centrality of monitoring and evaluation to educational development and innovation have been greatly reinforced by the educational model which has been consistently promulgated in recent years by the Government through the agencies of the Manpower Services Commission (now the Training Agency (TA)), the Further Education Unit (FEU) and increasingly the DES. This model is one which conceptualizes education essentially as a management task. The model is a *technical rational* one in which aims, methods and outcomes are conceived as being logically and operationally separable stages in a cyclic process. In this process monitoring and evaluation constitute a feedback loop between aims and outcomes to ensure progressive educational development and improvement. Third, the consequences of the Education Reform Act give the function of monitoring and evaluation a pre-eminent position within the new administrative apparatus which is coming into being.

Monitoring and evaluation is increasingly seen therefore as a specialist field requiring the possession of the relevant expertise. The effect of being regularly engaged in evaluation helps to develop an expertise which is both substantial and authoritative. HM inspectors, by the mere fact that they are continually observing learning wherever it occurs, have an individual and collective experience which is unrivalled. There is no other group of educationists, whether teachers, advisers or teacher educators and researchers, which so frequently encounters the reality of learning in all its variety of form and location. This experience continually refreshes and extends inspectors' knowledge of educational provision and sets it within a context wider than that of a single institution, or LEA. HMI has a unique national perspective which it is difficult to see could be acquired in any other way. The experience ensures that the practice of educational description and judgment is continually exercised.

Despite all of this expertise, however, we know surprisingly little about how the practice of inspection is actually carried out. It is true that we have access to the outcomes of inspection in the form of published reports and also knowledge of the broad organizational types of inspection. What is not generally available is detailed knowledge of how inspectors, both individually and in teams, go about the tasks of collecting and interpreting data and transforming them into descriptive accounts and considered educational judgments. The assumptions, criteria, techniques, and evaluation models on which the practice of inspection rests are unclear. Inspection is at the same time both the most influential means of educational evaluation and also the least known.

We have already noted the surprising absence of authoritative accounts of inspection within the literature of educational evaluation. This in turn reflects a lack of relationship between inspectors and those — mainly academics and researchers — who have contributed to this literature. There is little indication in the past of much dialogue having taken place between the two communities. This is unfortunate since it has led to a somewhat limited conception of educational evaluation in the academic community. It has also not helped inspectors in developing an adequate conceptual basis for their practice which is open to public scrutiny.

The literature of evaluation is replete with a variety of apparently contending models and approaches. These may, however, be located on a continuum with a concern for the measurement of quantifiable measures at one end, and an emphasis on rich naturalistic description at the other. Inspection tends to be implicitly regarded as lying towards the latter end of this continuum.

> HMIs and local authority inspectors and advisers adopt a style which does not aim to evaluate through the use of quantifiable measures but through mainly descriptive and 'connoisseurship' modes of evaluation (Kogan, 1986).

The two ends of the evaluation continuum define contrasting paradigms of profound significance not only for educational research and evaluation but for science and the nature of knowledge generally. These paradigms — the *naturalistic* and *positivist* — can be summarized succinctly in terms of the positions which each adopt on a number of issues. Compared to the positivist paradigm the naturalistic paradigm holds that:

— there are multiple constructed realities which can only be studied holistically rather than a single tangible reality 'out there' capable of analysis into discrete and independent variables and processes;

— in an enquiry the observer and the observed are interactive and inseparable and not independent of each other;

— the aim of an enquiry is to identify working hypotheses which describe the individual case rather than laws and principles which are true anywhere and at any time;

— all entities correspond to a state of mutual simultaneous shaping rather than to a series of discrete causes and effects;

— all enquiry is inevitably value-bound rather than value-free (Lincoln and Guba, 1985, pp. 36–38).

I suggest that the practice of inspection can be better understood in terms of the naturalistic paradigm rather than the positivist. Inspections are essentially enquiries of natural settings (such as schools in operation) which: unfold as data are collected and interpreted rather than following a totally predetermined design; tend to use qualitative approaches close to those of everyday life (observing, talking etc.) more than specialized quantitative methods; are able to utilize tacit knowledge; involve a close relationship with respondents (teachers and to an extent pupils); express their findings in terms of the particulars of the situation and report in something close to a case-study mode.

The methods of inspectors are similar in many ways to other field researchers working within the naturalistic tradition such as ethnographers and anthropologists. However, there is one very important respect in which the fieldwork of inspectors differs from that of these other field workers. The latter typically spend weeks or months, if not years in the field studying a particular institution, group or culture. In contrast inspectors typically spend a few days on a particular inspection (five days in a school or college during a full inspection by HMI). This time-constraint is a major distinguishing feature of the evaluation activities of inspectors and other educational practitioners. Such a very short period in the field is close to the notion of *condensed fieldwork* as originally introduced by Walker (1974) and developed to some extent in practice by Stenhouse (1982). Fieldwork carried out within such a short time-scale would be expected to affect significantly the methods of collecting and interpreting data.

In other words, inspection is a modified form of naturalistic enquiry which as yet lacks a publicly formulated conceptual framework and a codified repertory of methods and techniques. A related issue is the problem of judging the trustworthiness of the findings of naturalistic, enquiries in general and inspections in particular. The trustworthiness of evaluations in the positivist tradition is judged by reference to notions of objectivity, reliability and validity. These notions however are difficult to reconcile with the underpinning assumptions of naturalistic enquiry and are therefore not wholly appropriate for this methodological approach. It has to be admitted that as yet there is no general agreement on the criteria for judging the trustworthiness of findings from naturalistic enquiries, although Lincoln and Guba (1985) and Hutchinson *et al.* (1988) are among those who have made some useful suggestions. One technique which has been consistently recommended in qualitative research and evaluation and which is used — at the very least intuitively — in inspections is that of *triangulation*. In brief this is the process of corroborating an observation or judgment by drawing on evidence from more than one source (for example, observation, interviews, questionnaires and documents).

Establishing credibility for inspection as a means of generating educational knowledge will not necessarily be easy. This is because the positivist tradition continues to flourish in government bureaux, both local and national, and tends to represent a persistent cast of thinking when politicians, administrators and others concern themselves with issues of evaluation. Indeed this tendency has been substantially reinforced in recent years by the Government's implicit commitment to a philosophy of 'scientific management'. It would therefore be wise to make the whole process of inspection much more open to public scrutiny than it is at present. This would certainly involve making available accounts of how inspections are carried out that go beyond the usual specification of types and organizational arrangements to include details of *how* data are collected, interpreted and subsequently transformed into individual and collective descriptions and judgments.

Public confidence is also likely to be enhanced if assurance can be given that the techniques and methods used have been *systematically* developed within an inspectorate. This might mean inspectorates making public details of their training programmes for both new and experienced inspectors. It may also be wise to introduce a system for auditing the process and outcomes of inspection. Such a procedure has been suggested for naturalistic enquiries (Lincoln and Guba, 1985) although it does not appear to have been applied in the case of inspections. An audit could be carried out either during an inspection or after its completion. The auditor would need access to all documentation including the field notes and other records of individual inspectors. It would clearly be impractical for every inspection to be audited. Inspections might however be sampled periodically for internal audit by having one member of the inspection team fulfilling the auditor function. External audit might take place less frequently and could be carried out by a member of a different inspectorate or by someone who was a respected authority in the evaluation field and knowledgeable about naturalistic methods.

The final major criterion of credibility considered here is that of *usefulness*. The justification for evaluation of any type — inspection included — is that it should be useful. In particular the results of an inspection should be useful in providing knowledge and judgments to the institution or programme inspected to help confirm its strengths, remedy any weaknesses and further its development. At least two prerequisites are implied. The findings of the inspection must be reported with minimal delay following its completion. An inspection is a snapshot of an educational entity which is not static but which changes with time. If reporting is excessively delayed then the significance of the findings can diminish dramatically. However, given the careful scrutiny which a printed report requires (particularly if, as in the case of HMI reports, it is freely available to the public), some delay is inevitable. This is compensated for in most inspections by ensuring that relevant staff receive a detailed oral report at the conclusion of the inspection. Moreover, in the case of the inspection of schools or colleges, a similar report will also be made to the governing body as soon after the inspection as possible. The general aim is that the oral report should be sufficiently detailed for there to be no 'surprises' when the full published version appears in due course. Speedy feedback is also necessary as an act of courtesy to those inspected and as a means of ensuring that motivation and commitment to change is maintained.

The second prerequisite is that the report should be such that the findings of the inspection are presented in a form in which they can be clearly understood and acted upon. This necessity has implications for the length, structure and language of the report. The task of preparing reports meeting such criteria is one which requires of the tyro inspector much practice and guidance from more experienced colleagues. It is an aspect on which HMI in particular lavish much care and effort.

An inspection report should also be useful in other ways. It should have the potential to assist the general development of the *class* of educational enterprise which it describes. In other words it should contribute to the knowledge base on which the LEA (and perhaps the DES) might draw in order to inform their strategic planning of particular sectors and aspects of education. Of course a single inspection report (on, say, a particular secondary school) is unlikely *of itself* to assist in this general way. However when considered with the findings of reports of other secondary schools then issues, concerns and suggestions for development may become apparent. This kind of aggregation of findings from many individual inspections is frequently carried out by HMI and results in major reports on aspects of national educational provision. An important example is the study of secondary schools (DES, 1988b) which is a compilation based on the inspection of 185 secondary schools during the period 1982–86. Such reports, in full and summary forms, are available to LEAs and their institutions as well as to the educational and general media. The findings of inspection reports are thus widely disseminated and become part of a general corpus of knowledge of potential use to a variety of groups of educationists. Information to educational planners in the DES is not only provided through the vehicle of published reports. HMI, for example, will offer much of the advice gained through inspection by internal reports and memos as well as, of course, by word of mouth.

Another important use of inspection is to increase the general public's understanding and awareness of educational issues. Only a minority of the public will have direct access to actual inspection reports. However the media coverage given to HMI reports, which is often considerable, ensures that some understanding of their findings enters into the public consciousness.

There are thus three aspects of the potential usefulness of inspection:

— to help the development of individual institutions, programmes etc.;
— to contribute to a knowledge base for use by policy-makers, planners and managers;
— to contribute to the general public's understanding and awareness of educational matters and issues.

All three of these benefits should be possible outcomes from the inspections carried out by advisers within individual LEAs. Indeed it could be argued that the benefits might be even more apparent within an LEA context where issues are more specific, the locality and community of interest more defined, and the resources for follow-up action and implementation close at hand.

Judging the usefulness of inspection in the sense of discerning unequivocal effects on institutions, programmes, policy and practice is immensely difficult. It is therefore not surprising to find that the attempt to assess the value of inspection has been through the use of the Select Committee, special enquiry, and the organizational review. There is inevitably an element of faith about justifying any major aspect of social policy — much depends on its match with the dominant political ideology. Government policies in education are premised on the delegation of management responsibilities from LEAs to schools and colleges. Such a devolved system predicates a strong system of accountability. That accountability is to be exercised through an enhanced programme of inspection.

> The Department's wish is to see HMI and local inspectors co-operating more closely so that the country will benefit from an inspection service which . . . [will] identify and report on the quality of teaching and the standards of learning.
>
> The joint service — national and local — will see inspection, in all its forms, as an instrument for promoting good education and taking action to improve matters where necessary (Hancock, 1988, p. 4).

## Inspection and Other Approaches to Evaluation

I have suggested that there are several criteria for judging the credibility of educational knowledge generated by inspection. In brief they are:

— impartiality and independence;
— educational experience;
— monitoring and evaluation experience;
— acceptance by practitioners and the public of the methods used;
— usefulness of the outcomes of the methods used.

These same criteria should be among those used in assessing any other method which claims to generate credible educational knowledge. One such method is *school self-evaluation (SSE)* which was adopted by some LEAs in the late 1970s and early 1980s. How does SSE measure up against the above criteria? As already noted, reassuring the public about its concern for impartiality and independence is inherently more difficult for any approach which involves people evaluating the effects of their own efforts. Furthermore, the methods of self-evaluation are probably less well understood generally than even those of inspection. On the question of usefulness of its outcomes it seems that SSE is likely to be most effective where the concern is to further the development of the individual institution rather than to satisfy issues of accountability (Clift *et al.*, 1987). It is also difficult to see for SSE, at least as practised thus far, how its findings could be aggregated to provide a knowledge base capable of informing either LEA-wide planning tasks or the community's awareness of the general state of educational provision within its bailiwick. Implications for some of the other criteria above are suggested in the comment which concludes a major research study of SSE schemes:

> School self-evaluation requires a highly professional teaching force, trained in the skills of institutional review, aware and confident of their own professionality, possessed of the high morale necessary to seek for constant improvement in the quality of the education which they offer and confident of the support in this from other stakeholders in education. The institutionalization of SSE requires a different apportionment of teachers' time and energy than that pertaining in most schools at the present time. Whether its constant application to schools as they are by teachers as they are would lead to these remains a matter of doubt (Clift *et al.*, 1987: 210).

Despite this somewhat cautious assessment of the potential of SSE it is likely, *faute de mieux*, to be a component in the LEA-wide evaluation programmes that the 1988 Act will require. This is because the scope of the evaluation task is so great that inspection alone, even 'inspection in its forms', will be unable to tackle it. The implication of financial delegation and its associated budgetary cycle is that the performance of schools and colleges will need to be reviewed on an annual basis. There is no way that can be accomplished for every institution by relying solely on inspection — even if advisers concentrated their activities on institutional inspection, and their complement was very substantial increased. In addition, there are other evaluation tasks which will make demands on advisers' time, e.g. in-service programmes. It is also doubtful, even in LEAs which have established separate inspectorates, whether inspectors will work on inspections for the whole of their time.

A mixed evaluation approach is therefore likely in which SSE, inspection, and the use of performance indicators (PIs) are the main components. Such a blend was foreshadowed in the influential report by Coopers and Lybrand (1988) which advised the Government on the feasibility of LMS.

> The other side of the coin of greater delegated authority is the need for monitoring and accountability for the uses to which the greater freedom is put. We suggest there should be three mechanisms: the use of performance indicators, an enhanced role for the advisers/inspectorates and the production of an annual report on the school's performance. (op cit: 31)

However that might work out in practice — and different variants are possible — it is essential that the whole is co-ordinated by the LEA, through its advisory service, to form a coherent programme. Such a programme might involve advisers in the following tasks:

1 Working with institutions to develop an economical system of SSE incorporating performance indicators which is capable of yielding an annual report on performance;

2 Training staff in the use of such a system and giving accreditation to schools and colleges as SSE institutions;

3 When such a system is established, monitoring the quality of SSE by regular 'audit' checks on an annual sampling basis;

4 Developing a cycle of more intensive monitoring and evaluation on an annual sample of institutions through inspections and perhaps joint exercises involving advisers and institutional staff;

5 Maintaining, where possible with incorporation within 4 above,

a regular programme of inspections of individual departments and other aspects of institutional organization and provision;

6 Inspecting other elements of educational provision such as programmes, projects and services in accordance with LEA priorities.

Such an arrangement would help to ensure that the regular monitoring of institutions was maintained within a programme which gave due regard to the evaluation of other features of the education service. It is important to ensure that adequate knowledge is produced about the nature and quality of educational provision across the LEA as a whole. To put it simply, it is necessary to know not only how an individual institution is doing generally but also how specific aspects of provision are faring throughout the LEA, for example, 'what is the quality of mathematics teaching in primary schools?'

The development of a sound core of inspection within an LEA programme of evaluation will serve an additional purpose. The more systematically methods of inspection can be developed, practised and understood, the more likely they are to influence other less well-established time-constrained approaches to evaluation including SSE.

Maybe in the very long term the necessity for inspection will diminish, leaving a truly enlightened educational establishment and public able to carry out the functions of evaluation without the need for an external agency. Such a millenial prospect is not yet in sight. For the time being inspection will continue to play a vital part in the evaluation strategy of any LEA that is serious about addressing the issue of educational quality.

## Note

1 This chapter was written in 1990. Since then the Education (Schools) Act 1992 has become law. As a result from September 1993, the inspection responsibilities formerly exercised by HMI and LEA inspectors have been fundamentally changed.
2 The Inspection Methodologies for Education and Training (IMET) Project was funded by the Training Agency from January 1989 to October 1990. It was based in the Centre for Qualitative and Quantitative Studies in Education (QQSE), Division of Education, the University of Sheffield.
3 This return was subsequently discontinued a year or so after its introduction.

## References

CLIFT, P.S., NUTTALL, D.L. and McCORMICK, R. (1987) *Studies in School Self-Evaluation*, London, Falmer Press.

COOPERS and LYBRAND (1988) *Local Management of Schools: A Report to the Department of Education Science*, London, HMSO.

DAY, P. and KLEIN, R. (1990) *Inspecting the Inspectorates*, York, Joseph Rowntree Trust.

DES (1988a) *Education Reform Act: Local Management of Schools*, Circular 7/88, London, DES.

DES (1988b) *Secondary Schools*: An Appraisal by HMI, London, HMSO.

DES (1989a) *The Education (School Curriculum and Related Information) Regulations*, Circular 14/89, London, DES.

DES (1989b) *Standards in Education 1987–88: A Report by HMI*, London, DES.

GRAY, J. and HANNON, V. (1986) 'HMI Interpretation of Schools' Exam Results', *Journal of Educational Policy*, 1, 1, pp. 23–33.

HANCOCK, D. (1988) 'Speech to the NAIEA Executive' Supplement to *Perspective: The Journal for Advisers and Inspectors*, 5.

HUTCHINSON, B., HOPKINS, D. and HOWARD, J. (1988) 'The Problem of Validity in the Qualitative Evaluation of Categorically Funded Curriculum Development Projects', *Educational Research*, 30, 1, pp. 54–64.

KOGAN M. (1986) *Education Accountability: An Analytic Overview*, London, Hutchinson.

LAWTON, D. and GORDON, P. (1987) *HMI*, London, Routledge & Kegan Paul.

LINCOLN, Y.S. and GUBA, E.G. (1985) *Naturalistic Inquiry*, Beverley Hills, Sage.

MARDER, J.V. and JOHNSON, J.R.V. (1988) *British Educational Thesaurus*, Leeds, Leeds University Press.

SECRETARY OF STATE (1988) *Speech to the SEO*, London, DES Press Office.

SCHON, D.A. (1983) *The Reflective Practitioner*, London, Temple Smith.

STENHOUSE, L. (1982) 'The Conduct, Analysis, and Reporting of Case Study in Educational Research and Evaluation', in McCORMICK, R. (Ed.) *Calling Education to Account*, London, Heinemann, pp. 261–73.

STILLMAN, A.B. (1989) 'Institutional Evaluation and LEA Advisory Services', *Research Papers in Education*, 4, 2, pp. 3–27.

STILLMAN, A.B. and GRANT, M. (1989) *The LEA Adviser — A Changing Role*, Windsor, NFER-Nelson.

WALKER, R. (1974) 'The Conduct of Educational Case-Study: Ethics, Theory and Procedures', in McDONALD, B. and WALKER, R. (Eds) *Innovation, Evaluation Research and the Problem of Control*, Safari Interim Papers, Norwich, CARE, University of East Anglia.

WILCOX, B. (1991) *Time-Constrained Evaluation: A Practical Approach For LEAs and Schools*, London, Routledge.

WOLF, R.M. (1987) 'Educational Evaluation: the State of the Field', *International Journal of Education Research*, 11, 1, pp. 1–143.

Part Two

# Educational Research and Evaluation for Policy and Practice: Some Empirical Studies

# 7    Local and National Evaluation

*Christopher Pole*

## Introduction

In recent years, evaluation of one kind or another has become an integral part of teaching and education. While as Sikes (1989) points out, evaluation is an activity in which teachers necessarily engage in order that they may do their job efficiently and effectively, evaluation since the early 1980s has frequently been targeted at particular initiatives and developments in education. For example, the Technical and Vocational Education Initiative (TVEI), Records of Achievement, General Certificate of Secondary Education (GCSE), Grant Related In-Service Training (GRIST) and Local Education Authority Training Grants (LEATGS) have all been the focus of evaluation activities at national and local levels and in some cases at both.

Evaluation of these various initiatives may have been justified to the evaluated in terms of the formative development of the initiative and long-term benefits for education. In several cases, however, participation in evaluation exercises was made a condition of the receipt of government funding for participation in the initiative by the local education authority (LEA). This bond between funding and evaluation has produced a particular kind of relationship between the evaluator and the evaluated, one which Sikes (1989) sees in terms of greater 'governmental and societal demand for educational accountability'. LEAs were forced to accept evaluation in order to receive cash and in so doing a number of questions have arisen about the relationship of the evaluators and the evaluated. For example, were national and local evaluations in TVEI and Records of Achievement designed to help advance and develop the initiatives, to disseminate good practice or were they a means by which agents of the Department of Education and Science (DES) and the Manpower Services Commission (MSC) (now the Training Agency, TA) could keep track of what was happening to their cash? Furthermore, did the evaluation–cash nexus place the evaluator in an impossible role between central government and LEAs which meant not only that the scope of his/her evaluation was closely directed by its funders, but also that any findings of the evaluation were likely to be bland and of little use? For example, in the case of TVEI, schools and LEAs may have been keen to present a positive picture of the initiative to the MSC, who in turn were also concerned to present a positive view of what was seen by some to be a politically motivated departure in education (see Dale, 1990; McCulloch, 1987). In this context, could evaluators, whether national or local, ever be more than messengers or go-betweens of glad tidings?

This chapter examines some of the issues relating to the kinds of formal evaluation described above. By drawing on my personal experiences both as a national and a local evaluator,[1] I shall draw comparisons between these two different kinds of evaluation in the specific context of TVEI and Records of Achievement.

## Some Definitions

By the term formal evaluation I refer to those evaluations which are conducted by professional evaluators whose main occupation is usually the business of evaluation and/or research. I am not concerned, therefore, with evaluation conducted by participants, self-evaluation, although I do recognize that this is an important form of evaluation in schools.

By the term national evaluation I refer to those evaluations where the remit is for evaluation across an entire initiative, usually on a country-wide basis. In such cases the evaluation is usually funded by the organization which is funding and promoting the initiative, for example, the DES or the Training Agency. By local evaluation I refer to evaluation which is conducted at a local level, for example for an individual local education authority. In such cases, the local evaluator is usually engaged by the local authority and the contract of evaluation is agreed between the LEA and the evaluator.

From the definitions of the two types of evaluations it is clear that both local and national evaluation involve a contractual relationship between the evaluator and a managing body responsible for the evaluated. In national evaluations the managing body may be a government department; in local evaluations this would usually be the LEA. At the heart of the contractual relationship is the question of funding. In the case of TVEI the national evaluation was funded directly by the Man-power Services Commission (MSC) who were also responsible for funding the initiative as a whole. A contract was held, therefore, between NFER and MSC. For the local evaluation of TVEI and of Records of Achievement, however, the evaluation contract was held between the organization responsible for conducting the research (for example the university) and the local education authority for whom the evaluation was being conducted.

A proportion of the funds received by the LEA for the develop-ment of TVEI and Records of Achievement from central government were required to be designated to local evaluation. In this sense, fund-ing for the national and local evaluations came ultimately from the same source. The nature of the contract and the conditions under which LEAs received central government funds, however, meant that local and national evaluators conducted their work for different audiences.

As part of the criteria for LEAs to be accepted by the MSC for inclusion in the TVEI pilot scheme and to receive funds, they were required to outline the nature of the local evaluation as part of their original proposal and to state who would conduct it. The MSC also specified that a minimum of 1 per cent of the funding which the LEA received for TVEI should be spent by the LEA on local evaluation. This amount actually became the norm, which meant that in many cases local evaluations were conducted on what was regarded as a shoe-string budget (Fitzgibbon, 1986). As a result the kinds of evaluation activities in which local evaluators were able to engage sometimes amounted to little more than a crude survey or a series of HMI-style visits to TVEI schools.[2]

While the choice of TVEI and Records of Achievement local evaluators was left to the discretion of the LEA, guidelines from the funding bodies made clear that evaluators must be experienced in the practice and methodology of evaluation. With both initiatives most LEAs turned to their local university or polytechnic, but some con-ducted internal evaluations and others seconded teachers or LEA staff to universities to conduct the evaluation under supervision of a re-search centre or a department (Jeffrey, 1986).

With both TVEI and Records of Achievement, local and national evaluations were conducted more or less simultaneously.[3] In the case of TVEI however, many local evaluations were organized and were underway before the national evaluation teams were appointed and work could commence. Although local and national TVEI evaluators tried to keep each other informed of their activities, avoiding where possible duplication of effort and at the very least ensuring that they didn't turn up in the same school on the same day, there were some clashes of interest. Many schools which had been the subject of local and national evaluation complained of being 'evaluated to death' and if nothing else, TVEI produced a cohort of pupils who were adept at completing questionnaires!

In order to qualify for funding, however, all LEAs had to agree to cooperate with the national evaluation in addition to their own local evaluation. The initiative demanded, therefore, at least two levels of evaluation and there was little an LEA or a school could do to avoid being under the microscope if it wanted to keep its TVEI cash.

## The Role of Evaluation: Two Cases

In the case of TVEI and Records of Achievement, elaborate and expensive mechanisms of evaluation were employed. The organization of these evaluations raises a series of important questions about the purpose of evaluation, what it might achieve and the relationship between evaluators and evaluated. I wish to consider some of these issues, again with examples from TVEI and Records of Achievement, and in the first instance to consider the fundamental question of what evaluation's role is.

A useful general definition of evaluation is put forward by Sikes (1989). Once a TVEI local evaluator herself, Sikes draws on the work of Simons (1987) and McCormick and James (1983) to suggest the evaluator's aim is, 'to reveal educational possibilities, to understand as fully as possible what is going on and to reflect the situation back to those involved in it' (p. 141). If these objectives are seen as laudable for all evaluation, both national and local, then questions need to be asked about the capacity of both types of evaluation to fulfil the aims of providing a full understanding of the initiatives and reflecting the situation back to those involved in it. Moreover, it is interesting to consider whether, in the case of TVEI at least, the scale of the national evaluation actually precluded such aims.

In the case of TVEI there was a requirement that the national evaluation should reflect developments in all LEAs included in the pilot phase of the initiative. During the period of my involvement with this evaluation there were seventy-two such LEAs spread throughout England and Wales.[4] Implicit in the term 'national evaluation' and explicit in the contract between the NFER and the MSC was that the evaluation should cover all areas of the country, and indeed geographical diversity was one of the principal criteria in identifying LEAs where field work was to be conducted. With seventy-two LEAs spread throughout the length and breadth of England and Wales, data collection consequently involved several hundred schools, many thousands of pupils and several thousand teachers. LEA personnel and parents were also included in the evaluation. In addition, a wide-scale study of employers and their representatives likely to have contact with TVEI pupils was conducted (see Sims, 1989). For this huge exercise which was scheduled to be conducted over a period of four years, the NFER evaluation team, when at full strength, numbered only five.[5]

The methods employed by the team were a combination of qualitative and quantitative. Extensive travelling was required to achieve the required level of geographical diversity. For example, the team interviewed every project coordinator, interviewed school coordinators and TVEI teachers as far apart as Cumbria and Cornwall, held group discussions with TVEI pupils in many different locations, and interviewed employers from a variety of local labour markets. All of this more qualitative work occurred alongside large-scale surveys of pupils, heads, teachers, parents, school and LEA coordinators. An excerpt from my diary from 1986 reveals the pace of the data collection and shows how much travelling was involved:

For a week in March 1986:

Monday: Attended a meeting in Manchester arranged by the MSC to enable local and national evaluators to meet and discuss strategies.

Tuesday: Interviewed staff and pupils at a school in Leicester.

Wednesday: Interviewed LEA personnel in North Tyneside.

Thursday: AM — interviews at County Hall, Durham. PM — interviewed project coordinator in Newcastle.

Friday: Office (Slough) writing up fieldnotes.

Although all weeks were not as busy as this one, many were. The point of recalling these activities is to demonstrate the nature of data collection in this national exercise. Over a period of three days I visited four different TVEI schemes, seeking information on what were often complex management structures.[6] With such a tight schedule, little contextual data could be gathered. With seventy-two LEAs to evaluate, little was known about the authorities or schools before arriving. There was little opportunity to collect data from more than one source or to observe the things described and discussed during interviews.

In most cases, the one visit to the LEA was the only opportunity for contextual data collection. We worked with agreed interview schedules in an attempt to bring some standardization to our collected data. One of the concerns of the evaluation was to balance quantitative and qualitative data. Interviews were deemed to produce qualitative data so we conducted many of them.

In order to draw out some of the differences which I experienced between local and national evaluation and which can probably be accounted for by the scope and the objectives of the two different exercises, I wish to consider briefly my work as a Records of Achievement local evaluator. This was conducted via an ethnographic study of one FE college's experience of introducing Records of Achievement. In practice the exercise was very contained. The pilot scheme involved just eight courses, a fairly well-knit group. Furthermore, the funding for the evaluation allowed me to spend one-quarter of my time on this project for a period of two years. During this time I was able to develop a close working relationship with several of the course tutors, with LEA personnel and a knowledge of many of the students on the courses. I also attended LEA and college meetings, and became a regular user of the staffroom. The fact that I spent a considerable amount of time in the college meant that I was able to gather a great deal of contextual data and to see Records of Achievement as part of the activities of the institution and not merely as an isolated event. The detailed interviews I conducted with staff and students together with observation work and the many informal conversations which can provide a rich source of data (see Burgess, 1988), allowed me to gather different perspectives on the initiative, to ask a whole range of questions of people in different positions and, most importantly, to observe not only the development of the Record of Achievement in terms of policy, but also the experience of it in terms of practice.

In methodological terms, these two evaluation projects are illustrative of insider (Records of Achievement) and outsider (TVEI) approaches to evaluation. With TVEI the national evaluators could never be more than visitors to a school or an LEA. In this sense, the relationship between evaluator and the evaluated was formal and tempered by the evaluator's need to collect information efficiently and quickly. The national evaluator, or the HMI in this context, must always be aware of the capacity of schools to put on their 'best behaviour' for the period of the visit. With the local evaluation of Records of Achievement, I was much more a part of the development. The frequency of my visits to the college, which did not adhere to a fixed timetable, and the open access I was afforded by college personnel, made the management of 'best behaviour' very difficult if not impossible in the context. While I was not regarded as a colleague by the evaluated, there was certainly greater opportunity for dialogue and for staff to feel that they were part of the evaluation rather than just the subjects of it.

## The Contribution of the Evaluations

Let us consider again Sikes' (1989) definition of the aim of evaluation: '. . . to understand as fully as possible what is going on'. One might now reasonably ask with such a hectic schedule and the need to cover so many LEAs, so many schools, so many miles, could the national evaluation ever fully understand what was going on? Or could it present little more than a cameo, a snapshot of the initiative? At the same time, however, one must also ask questions about my role as a local evaluator. For example, while one might argue that the opportunity to get to know and understand what was going on was far greater in the local evaluation, the questions of objectivity, of the capacity of the evaluator to distance him/herself from the evaluated are surely paramount. In many ways my presence in the college and the fact that I selected it for the evaluation exercise, make me a participant in the evaluation. The fact that the college received attention under the local evaluation may in itself have been a catalyst for development of Records of Achievement there. In this sense, 'to understand as fully as possible what is going on' requires the evaluator to be constantly aware of his or her influence on the development of the initiative and of his or her contribution to what was actually going on.

The debate would seem to be about the capacity of the two different kinds of evaluation to provide adequate pictures and analyses of the developments. On the one hand the national evaluation sought to provide an overview with the evaluator cast in the role of outsider. In terms of the local evaluation the evaluator was part of the development, an insider. However, MacDonald (1976) argues that clinical objectivity is beyond evaluators by the very nature of the methodology they employ which, as Sikes (1989) states, reflects their own philosophies and beliefs. The very fact that an evaluator is present will affect the initiative, but hopefully for the better. And perhaps more than this, her or his presence will encourage participants to step back to take a critical look at what they are doing. Contamination does inevitably occur but the evaluator must seek to make it positive contamination. In these terms, it would seem that the local evaluation had a greater capacity to make a positive or formative contribution to the development of the initiative being evaluated, than did the wide-scale national evaluation.

To make such a statement is to assume, however, that formative development of the initiatives was an aim of both types of evaluation. To examine this issue, and the role of evaluation in the case of TVEI and Records of Achievement, it is necessary to consider two general questions about the nature of local and national evaluation. First, are national evaluations, as McCabe (1987) says, so wide-ranging as to produce little more than broad-brush data and general overviews or aggregates which contribute little to the understanding of processes? Second, are local evaluations too narrow, limited and particular to contribute to policy and practice?

To answer these questions we need to consider the way in which evaluators report and the second of Sikes' (1989) statements which she draws from MacDonald (1981): '. . . to reflect the situation back to those involved in it'. Ultimately evaluations usually report to the funding bodies. With TVEI, NFER reported to the MSC and with Records of Achievement, CEDAR reported to the college and the LEA simultaneously. In the case of NFER, reports were received by civil servants at the MSC. Papers and reports, even papers for delivery at conferences, were despatched to the MSC who commented on or cleared the papers for more general publication. Information and material often took several months to reach teachers and other practitioners after leaving NFER. By the time information was fed back to those involved in the initiative, situations had changed, the initiative had moved on and evaluation reports were rarely useful to those from whom data had been collected.

In the local evaluation, reports were made to participants throughout the evaluation, and discussions with interested and involved personnel were common as the evaluation progressed. Participants were asked to comment on reports and on my work in general. They were also invited to submit written reports themselves which could contribute to the evaluation. As the evaluation progressed, my work fed into the development of Records of Achievement in the college on a regular basis.

Cronbach (1963) argued that the principal aim of evaluation should be to improve whatever was being evaluated. This formative approach to evaluation may be seen as an important aspect of the local evaluation work in Records of Achievement. The national evaluation of TVEI, however, was rarely seen as formative in terms which would enhance classroom practices by the evaluated or the evaluators. The fact that data were collected by the national evaluators for what were seen as essentially summative purposes and were not fed back to schools directly led to some tension at times between the national evaluators and the evaluated (Hopkins, 1986). The formative evaluation in TVEI came almost entirely through the local evaluators, as Hopkins (1986), himself a TVEI local evaluator, points out:

> The local evaluations are the main means through which TVEI can be improved. The local evaluations are essentially formative (i.e. they feed back information for the purpose of improving practice) and as each is tailored to its own scheme, then in theory they are the most fruitful way of improving the quality of TVEI. No other evaluation strategy in TVEI is so intimately concerned with improving the quality of the product.

However, is it fair to perceive formative evaluation only in terms of its contribution to the work of practitioners at school level? Indeed, while the NFER evaluation was essentially summative because of its scale, methodology and reporting procedures, it was, nevertheless, seen as formative in a management and policy orientated sense, as the team members pointed out in a paper given at the 1985 NFER Annual Conference (Stoney, Pole and Sims, 1985):

> The national evaluations, of which the NFER studies form one part, are seeking to take a broad long-term view of the initiative and its functioning, and are particularly concerned with meeting the information needs of policy-makers at national and local level. As such, they are able to act in a formative manner to the education and training services generally by providing a fund of multi-faceted data, upon which decisions regarding the future developments of TVEI projects, as well as the initiative as a whole, can be based (p. 11).

While such statements are a useful means of national evaluators justifying the inconvenience they cause to practitioners in terms of deferred gratification, stressing the long-term good which will come of their work, it may be that unless there is some more immediate pay-off, practitioners see such activities as time-wasting, an intrusion and of little use to their day-to-day practices. Furthermore, Sikes (1989) suggests that such approaches may be perceived as threatening. Moreover, if the emphasis in evaluation is placed on gathering facts to be used by government and policy-makers, then the evaluator may become little more than the medium for this information or, even as McCabe (1987) suggests, a means of policing the initiative. From the evaluator's perspective, a role for the evaluator merely as a collector of facts may mean that he or she becomes a mere technician (Finch, 1986), divorced from the decision-making process or the consequences of his or her work.

In terms of the TVEI national evaluation, I certainly felt at a distance from my work. Once reports were dispatched to MSC I recall feelings of relief, as though my responsibility for the evaluation ended there. The contractual obligation had been met; it was now the responsibility of the MSC to use the reports in a formative and developmental way, if they saw fit. In Finch's (1986) terms, I was merely a technician.

With the local evaluation of Records of Achievement the situation was quite different. Reports and my work in general were discussed throughout the course of the evaluation. Attendance at meetings at college and LEA level meant there was a dialogue about my work and the findings at a variety of different levels. In addition I was also regarded as a source of information about Records of Achievement and while I was concerned not to be seen as 'the expert' I did, nevertheless, pass on information or literature about developments in initiatives in different parts of the country if requested to do so. In many respects, my role seemed to fit with that identified by McCabe (1987) which cast the evaluator in a similar role to that of a management consultant. The capacity of the evaluator to make a formative contribution to the initiative, in this case, was clearly much greater.

## Conclusion

This chapter has highlighted some issues relating to local and national evaluation. My experience of both types of evaluation has led me to portray a more positive view of local evaluation in terms of the depth of understanding that it has the capacity to produce, and also its contribution to the development of the subject of the evaluation. However, I do not wish to dismiss national evaluation *per se* as being of little use. For example, the national evaluation of Records of Achievement produced two influential documents (PRAISE, 1987, 1988) which informed national policy statements on Records of Achievement

(RANSC, 1989) and were widely read among practitioners. Furthermore I know that all members of the NFER team (including myself) worked hard as national evaluators in the belief that our work was worthwhile. The subsequent failure of the national evaluation of TVEI to have any major impact on the extension of the initiative to all LEAs in England and Wales (TVEE) seems to have been more to do with the scale of the evaluation and the political need for TVEI to be successful than with failings on the part of NFER. Also, it would be easy from what I have said to believe that relationships between local evaluators and the evaluated are always cosy. This is certainly not the case. For example Nixon (1989), in a paper entitled 'What is Evaluation After the MSC?', reflects on his experience as a local evaluator for the Sheffield TVEI Scheme. He concludes that the contractual relationship which existed between him and the LEA and between the LEA and the MSC precluded effective evaluation which allowed him to ask real ethical questions about TVEI. As such he declares that: '. . . evaluation under MSC (and now the Training Agency) funding, runs the very real risk of becoming the mere tool of management'.

From my experience of these two kinds of evaluation, the nature of the evaluation contract seems to have been the key to the scope and scale of the work, the methodology and most importantly, the capacity for the evaluation to contribute to policy and practice. In the case of the TVEI national evaluation, 'covering the ground', getting the response rates and meeting MSC deadlines for reports seemed to become more important than providing information which would be useful to practitioners or understanding the initiative which we were evaluating. Moreover, the kind of information which the evaluation did yield to practitioners (see Stoney *et al.*, 1986; Hinckley *et al.*, 1987; Bridgewood *et al.*, 1988) may at best be seen as interesting, rather than useful, providing information on general trends within TVEI.

Sanday (this volume) discusses the relationship between evaluation and the role of the LEA. He outlines a number of points of potential tension which may exist between LEAs and external evaluators, one of which may arise from the fact that evaluation is a prerequisite for funding and as such LEAs are told to engage professional evaluators. Consequently, the evaluation may be seen as a means to an end, a necessary inconvenience tied to the release of cash. Surely this is to present a particularly negative view of evaluation which fails to recognize the positive contributions which it can make? However, it may be a view which is widely held among LEA staff.

To overcome such views, especially if evaluation at local and national level is to remain a feature of education, evaluators must look to the evaluated. They should listen to their concerns and to what they would regard as a useful outcome of the evaluation. This dialogue will help to identify an appropriate scope and methodology for the evaluation. At the same time, the evaluator should not be afraid to advise the evaluated on the kinds of information which would be useful. Those purchasing evaluation at a local level are, after all, buying skills and expertise which they may not have readily available. By doing this, the evaluators may be coming close to what MacDonald (1976) sees as their duty in a democratic society — to identify and consult interest groups and to furnish them with information which they would find useful and valuable.

Rather than the evaluator acting merely as messenger, a technician (Finch, 1986), or an inspector, I would advocate the role of evaluator in McCabe's (1987) terms as management consultant. He believes that the work of an evaluator is not the mere collating of information or description, however much insight this might involve. The key functioning of evaluation is the reviewing of what is happening, the identification of key concepts and the questions they give rise to. With this approach the evaluator has the capacity to become more than an inspector or a conveyor of information. The evaluator, through questioning of and critical dialogue with the evaluated, may make an important contribution to the initiative.

### Notes

1  The author was a member of the team of researchers at the National Foundation for Educational Research (NFER) responsible for conducting the national evaluation of the organization and operation of TVEI. More recently he has conducted one of the local evaluation projects for the Pilot Records of Achievement in Schools Evaluation Extension.
2  In some cases, local evaluations were conducted for a consortium of LEAs by the same university. Notably the Universities of Lancaster and Newcastle and the Open University arranged such a consortium.
3  Another example of this co-existence of national and local evaluation can be seen in the DES Lower Achieving Pupils Project (LAPP).
4  This figure represents the number of LEAs accepted as pilot schemes for the first and second rounds of the pilot initiative. In subsequent rounds the number included in the national evaluation increased.
5  Delays in initial recruitment and staff subsequently leaving to take up other posts meant that there were rarely five full-time members in post at any one time.
6  Data collection was further complicated by the teacher industrial action of 1985/86. Despite this, however, the team usually received cooperation from teachers and other personnel.

## References

BRIDGEWOOD, A., HINCKLEY, S., SIMS, S. and STONEY, S. (1988) *Perspectives on TVEI, NFER Evaluation Report 4*, Sheffield, Training Agency.

BURGESS, R.G. (1988) 'Conversations with a Purpose: The Ethnographic Interview in Educational Research', in BURGESS, R. (Ed.) *Studies in Qualitative Methodology, Volume 1, Conducting Qualitative Research*, London, JAI Press.

CRONBACH, L.J. (1963) 'Course Improvement through Evaluation', *Teacher College Record*, **64**, pp. 672–83.

DALE, R. (1990) (Ed.) *The TVEI Story: Policy and Preparation for the Workforce*, Milton Keynes, Open University Press.

FINCH, J. (1986) *Research and Policy. The Uses of Qualitative Methods in Social and Educational Research*, London, Falmer Press.

FITZGIBBON, C. (1986) 'The Roles of TVEI Local Evaluator', in HOPKINS, D. (Ed.) *Evaluating TVEI: Some Methodological Issues*, Cambridge, Cambridge Institute of Education.

HINCKLEY, S., POLE, C., SIMS, S. and STONEY, S. (1987) *The TVEI Experience: NFER Evaluation Report 2*, Sheffield Training, Agency.

HOPKINS, D. (Ed.) (1986) *Evaluating TVEI: Some Methodological Issues*, Cambridge, Cambridge Institute of Education.

JEFFREY, D. (1986) 'Professional Evaluation: Sheep in Wolf's Clothing', *Cambridge Journal of Education*, **16**, 2.

LAWTON, D. (1986) 'The Politics of Curriculum Evaluation', in LAWTON, D. (Ed.) *Politics of the School Curriculum*, London, Routledge & Kegan Paul.

MACDONALD, B. (1976) 'Evaluation and the Control of Education', in TOWNEY, D. (Ed.) *Curriculum Evaluation Today*, London, Macmillan.

MACDONALD, B. (1981) 'Interviewing in case study evaluation', *Phi, Delta Kappa CEDRE Quarterly*, **14**, 4.

McCABE, C. (1987) 'The External Evaluator — Inspector or Management Consultant?', in *Evaluation and Research in Education*, **1**, 1.

McCORMICK, R. and JAMES, M. (1983) *Curriculum Evaluation in Schools*, London, Croom Helm.

McCULLOCH, G. (1987) 'History and Policy: The Politics of the TVEI, in GLEESON, D. (Ed.) *TVEI and Secondary Education: A Critical Appraisal*, Milton Keynes, Open University Press.

NIXON, J. (1989) 'What is Evaluation After the MSC?' in BURGESS, R. (Ed.) *The Ethics of Educational Research*, London, Falmer Press.

PRAISE (1987) *Pilot Records of Achievement in Schools Evaluation, an Interim Report*, London, DES/Welsh Office.

PRAISE (1988) *Report of the Pilot Records of Achievement in Schools Evaluation*, London, DES/Welsh Office.

RANSC (1989) *Report of the Records of Achievement National Steering Committee*, London, DES/Welsh Office.

SIKES, P. (1989) 'De-Mystifying Evaluation', in WOODS, P. (Ed.) *Working for Teacher Development*, Dereham, Peter Francis.

SIMONS, H. (1987) *Getting to Know Schools in a Democracy: The Politics and Processes of Evaluation*, London, Falmer Press.

Christopher Pole

SIMS, D. (1989) *Leaving TVEI and Starting Work: Employment Processes and Employer Research*, Sheffield, Training Agency.
STONEY, S., POLE, C. and SIMS, S. (1985) 'Evaluating TVEI: Some Thoughts on the Project's First Year', in *Assessment and Evaluation. Proceedings of the 1985 NFER Conference*, Slough, NFER.
STONEY, S., POLE, C. and SIMS, S. (1986) *The Management of TVEI, NFER Evaluation Report 1*, Sheffield, Training Agency.

# 8 Evaluation for Policy: Rationality and Political Reality: The Paradigm Case of PRAISE?[1]

*Mary James*

## Argument

The message of this chapter is not very optimistic. In the light of my experience as an evaluator in an area of national policy, I am forced to acknowledge what I probably always knew deep down: that the classic definition of the role of evaluation as providing information for decision-makers (Cronbach, 1963; Stufflebeam *et al.*, 1971; Davis, 1981) is a fiction if this is taken to mean that policy-makers who commission evaluations are expected to make rational decisions based on the best (valid and reliable) information available to them. Policy-making is, by definition, a rational activity and political considerations will always provide convenient answers to awkward questions thrown up by research. Thus the ideal of rational decision-making based on information derived from research-based evaluation is probably illusory. The best that evaluators can hope to do, if they discover that their findings are at variance with the current political agenda, is to make public their evidence. This will give those who are affected by policy a chance to understand the real basis on which decisions are made, and to become aware of the alternatives, some of which may still be realized if there is a will to work in the interstices of policy, or towards changing the policy-makers by means of electoral procedures.

This is not a new idea. It is at the heart of the concept of 'democratic evaluation' (MacDonald, 1977; Simons, 1987) which regards evaluation as 'an information service to the community' underpinned by the basic value of an 'informed citizenry'. As such it is potentially

subversive of the hegemony of those with the most power to determine policy, which is tantamount to adopting a political (small 'p')
role itself. This vision of evaluation is a far cry from conceptions of a
value-free science, but it acknowledges an important dimension of the
contexts in which evaluators work and which acts as an inevitable and
powerful constraint on their work.

Although I came across the concept of democratic evaluation fifteen
years ago, it was only with direct result of my experience of policy
evaluation that I fully appreciated its import. The reality of the strength
of political imperative over the ability of research evidence to persuade
policy-makers was brought home to me especially forcefully simply
because the outlook for the Pilot Records of Achievement In Schools
Evaluation (PRAISE), with which I was involved, from 1985 to 1990
was so propitious. In many ways it promised to provide a model for
the way that evaluation could feed into policy-making, yet the fulfilment of this promise was undermined by changes in political priorities. As they say, 'a week is a long time in politics' and, except in the
most limited circumstances, the time-scale that evaluation demands
renders it relatively powerless to influence policy-making at the level
at which it is commissioned. Let me explain by way of a brief history.

### Evidence

In 1985 a team of researchers from the Open University School of
Education and Bristol University School of Education was commissioned by the Department of Education and Science and the Welsh
Office to evaluate progress and results in nine pilot schemes set up,
with the support of Education Support Grants, to develop records of
achievement in secondary schools.

In the preceding years, interest in records of achievement had been
stimulated in a number of ways. In 1938, 1943 and 1963, respectively,
the Spens, Norwood, and Newsom Reports had all commented on the
failure of school examination certificates to provide information about
the full range of pupils' experiences and achievements over ten years of
compulsory schooling. Indeed it was deplored that many pupils left
school with nothing at all to show for what they had done. The problem became even more acute with the proposal to raise the school
leaving age to 16 in 1973; after all, how could anyone expect youngsters to be well motivated if they received no recognition for the extra
time spent in school? These twin issues of motivation and recognition
of achievement were perceived as increasingly important by a growing

number of schools, local authorities and consortia, including examinations boards, who, by developing pupil profiles and records of achievement, sought to tackle the problem and provide more meaningful experiences for pupils, particularly those unlikely to achieve recognition for their efforts through the conventional examination route. In a period of approximately ten years, from the early 1970s to the early 1980s, these grass-roots developments grew into a substantial profiling and records of achievement movement, underpinned by a fairly coherent set of principles. Eventually it came to the attention of the Government (see Fairbairn, 1988, for an historical review, and Brown and Black, 1988, for more detail on the Scottish experience).

The interest taken by Sir Keith Joseph, a former Secretary of State for Education, in profiling and records of achievement (the two terms were often used interchangeably) was very much related to his particular interest in doing something for the 'bottom 40 per cent' of pupils, that is, those pupils who at the time were not expected to achieve GCE or CSE qualifications. Thus he pursued the idea of a government-sponsored records of achievement initiative alongside the Lower Attaining Pupils Programme (LAPP) and the first phase of the Technical and Vocational Education Initiative (TVEI). The first pronouncement to emerge from the Department of Education and Science (apart from an HMI survey in 1982) was a draft statement of policy on records of achievement which was subject to widespread consultation in 1983. While welcomed in principle, teachers and educationists pressed for substantial changes; in particular they sought to shake off the 'less able only label' that had been adopted in the 1970s but which was now ideologically unacceptable. The result of this consultation process was a much-revised and well-received Statement of Policy which was published by the DES and Welsh Office in 1984.

The stated intention of the Secretaries of State in 1984 was that a framework of national policy for records of achievement should be established by the end of the decade, and that these national arrangements should be designed to meet four main purposes:

1 *Recognition of achievement.* Records and recording systems should recognize, acknowledge and give credit for what pupils have achieved and experienced, not just in terms of results in public examinations but in other ways as well. They should do justice to pupils' own efforts and to the efforts of teachers, parents, ratepayers and taxpayers to give them a good education.

2 *Motivation and personal development.* They should contribute to pupils' personal development and progress by improving their

motivation, providing encouragement and increasing their awareness of strengths, weaknesses and opportunities.

3 *Curriculum and organization.* The recording process should help schools to identify the all-round potential of their pupils and to consider how well their curriculum, teaching and organization enable pupils to develop the general, practical and social skills which are to be recorded.

4 *A document of record.* Young people leaving school or college should take with them a short summary document of record which is recognized and valued by employers and institutions of further and higher education. This should provide a more rounded picture of candidates for jobs of courses than can be provided by a list of examination results, thus helping potential users to decide how candidates could best be employed, or for which jobs, training schemes or courses they are likely to be suitable (DES, 1984, para. 11).

In fulfilment of these purposes the Secretaries of State expected that, among other things, records of achievement systems should:

— cover a pupil's progress and activities across the whole educational programme of the school, both in the classroom and outside the school as well (para. 16);
— concentrate on positive aspects of a young person's school career and personal qualities (para. 13);
— closely involve pupils in the recording process by giving them an opportunity to make a contribution of their own (para. 36) and by involving them in a process of regular teacher–pupil dialogue (para. 16);
— ensure that the summary document of record becomes the property of pupils who would be free to decide whether or not to show it to prospective employers and others (para. 40);
— be based on national guidelines which would provide for a common format for the summary documents of record and establish appropriate forms of validation and accreditation (para. 31). This was regarded as essential if records of achievement were to have credibility in the eyes of potential users (para. 33).

At this point little guidance was given concerning the relationship with other forms of internal recording and reporting to parents, although it was noted that these were important issues for consideration:

An issue which the pilot schemes will need to address is the relationship between the internal reporting, recording and dialogue discussed in this statement and the procedures for the end of term (or end of year) reports which schools send to parents. Also relevant are other reporting processes for parents or for careers purposes. It would clearly be neither sensible nor economic to treat all these activities as totally separate. There may be scope for improving the coverage of end of term reports, and these reports may form a valuable item of agenda for internal discussions between teacher and pupil (DES, 1984, para. 38).

Broad coverage and interactive processes were, therefore, seen to be key features to be developed in all recording and reporting systems.

On the basis of this 1984 policy statement, nine pilot schemes were set up involving twenty-two local education authorities and approximately 250 schools and colleges. In the first instance these were to run for three years from April 1985 to March 1988. At the same time the PRAISE national evaluation was established, with funding from the DES and Welsh Office, and a Records of Achievement National Steering Committee (RANSC) was convened. The latter was chaired by an Assistant Secretary at the DES and its membership included teachers, educationists, industrialists and examinations board representatives. RANSC was expected to 'steer, monitor and evaluate the pilot schemes' and 'to oversee the work of the professional evaluating team' (RANSC, 1989, p. 30). On the basis of the information received direct from the pilot schemes and from the national evaluation, RANSC was asked to

report to the Secretaries of State in the autumn of 1988 on the experience gained and on the implications for introducing records of achievement for all pupils in secondary schools in England and Wales, and to prepare draft national guidelines for such records and recording systems.

The work of independent evaluators was therefore integrated into the structures for policy-making in a way that has rarely been the case. (It also contrasts sharply with the introduction of the National Curriculum which has been subject to no comparable piloting or evaluation.) Indeed the introduction of a national system for records of achievement was to be the culmination of a lengthy and thorough process of piloting, evaluation, deliberation, recommendation, consultation and legislation. However, a close examination of the *actual* sequence of events reveals that new circumstances, notably the provisions of the 1988 Education Reform Act, significantly altered the predicted course of policy-making with respect to records of achievement.

1984
- DES policy statement on records of achievement.
- Invitation to LEAs and consortia to bid to become pilot schemes with the support of ESG.
- Invitation to research institutions to tender for the national evaluation.

1985
- Funding of nine pilot schemes at a cost of £6.75 million in England and an additional sum for Wales (1985 prices).
- Funding of national evaluation (PRAISE) at a cost of £239,000 (1985 prices).
- Initiation of parallel HMI exercise to monitor progress in pilot schemes (to report directly to the Secretaries of State).
- RANSC convened to monitor, steer, and receive reports from pilot schemes and PRAISE.

1986
- RANSC received interim reports from pilot schemes and PRAISE.
- DES published introductory leaflet for teachers.

1987
- RANSC received interim reports from pilot schemes and PRAISE.
- PRAISE interim report published by Bristol and Open Universities.
- DES/WO published RANSC interim report and further leaflet for teachers.
- DES/WO conducted consultation exercise on the basis of the RANSC interim report.

1988
- RANSC received final reports from pilot schemes and PRAISE.
- PRAISE final report published by HMSO.
- HMI final report published by DES.
- RANSC reported to the Secretaries of State and offered draft national guidelines.
- Some pilot schemes and PRAISE funded for further development and evaluation of selected issues (until March 1990) — £2.4 million for pilot schemes and £108,000 for PRAISE (1988 prices).
- Records of Achievement Extension Steering Committee (RESC) set up to monitor and receive

reports from the national evaluation extension project (PRAISE B), but not in this instance to make policy recommendations itself.

1989
- RANSC report published by the DES/WO.
- PRAISE case-studies published in four volumes by Bristol University and the Open University.
- Secretary of State invited SEAC to consult on the findings of the RANSC report *in the light of requirements for reporting National Curriculum assessments under Section 22 of the Education Reform Act, 1988* (20 January).
- SEAC advised the Secretaries of State on the basis of consultation (13 July).
- Junior Minister of Education (Schools) announced arrangements for the preparation of Regulations concerning the recording and reporting of achievement in relation to National Curriculum assessments and the setting up of a primary school project (16 August).
- PRAISE B interim report submitted to RESC and subsequently published by Bristol University.
- TVEI Unit of the Training Agency issued draft guidance on records of achievement for those managing TVEI (5 December).

1990
- Publication of draft Statutory Orders and proposed accompanying Circular under Section 22 Regulations: Information on Individual Pupils' Achievements (5 January)
- DES/WO Consultation on draft Statutory Orders and Circular (by 31 March)
- Publication of the Statutory Instrument (No. 1381) for The Education (Individual Pupils' Achievements) (Information) Regulations 1990 and of the accompanying Circular 8/90 on Records of Achievement. Guidance for those managing TVEI published concurrently (10 July).
- Final report of the national evaluation extension project (PRAISE B) sent to ministers (October) for approval for publication by HMSO in early 1991.
- Publication by SEAC of non-statutory guidance on Records of Achievement in Primary Schools (Bath project) (November 1990).

- Secretary of State for Education (Clarke) announced the intention to launch a core format for a National Record of Achievement (NRA), initially for school leavers at 16+ (13 November).
- Core format of National Record put out for quick consulation by Department of Employment (prime mover) and DES (5 December for 13 January 1991).

1991
- DES issued for consultation a standard format for reports at KS 1–3 (17 January).
- Publication of PRAISE B Report (22 February).
- 'Launch' by Department of Employment of the National Record of Achievement (27 February). Sample to be sent to each secondary school. Intended to be used with school leavers in July 1991.
- DES published model format for school reports at KS 1–3 (20 March).

1992
- Prime Minister announced (23 January) handover of NRA to NCVQ, to be completed by 1 April.
- DES published Circular 5/92 on 'Reporting Pupils' Achievements to Parents' and regulations, extending and superseding Circular 8/90. These required comparative information on NC assessment results in reports to parents.
- NCVQ published consultative document on Action Planning and the NRA (October) and invited responses by December.
- NRA development programme established by NCVQ involving 7 projects, most focusing on quality assurance (October).

1993
- Revised NRA format to be launched (September).[†]

1994
- Full arrangements for the national quality assurance of NRA implementation to be published (January).[†]

[†]   These are proposed but not available at the time of writing.

As this catalogue of events reveals, the delivery of reports from the main phase of work by PRAISE (1985–88) was timed to feed into the deliberations of RANSC. Moreover, since the codirectors of PRAISE were also members of that committee they were able to draw the attention of RANSC to items of evidence with a bearing on particular policy questions. The relationship between PRAISE and RANSC was therefore highly productive and PRAISE findings were able to inform the recommendations of RANSC in a very direct way. Indeed, a comparative content analysis of the PRAISE and RANSC reports reveals that the latter drew very substantially on the former, to the extent of quoting verbatim in many places.[2]

On the whole the RANSC report was well received and in his letter to the Secretary of State dated 13 July 1989, which accompanied the report of the consultation exercise, the Chairman of the School Examinations and Assessment Council recommended that RANSC-style records of achievement should be 'required for use with pupils across the age range 5–16' although he thought it would be undesirable to prescribe all the detailed content and procedures.

On the basis of this, one might expect that the eventual outcome of five years of piloting and evaluation — which has cost over ten million pounds of public money — and the report of an official committee, would be a national scheme for records of achievement, as more or less envisaged in the RANSC report. Although questions persisted concerning certain issues and matters of detail, the principles on which records of achievement schemes were founded achieved a remarkable degree of support. Despite this support, it soon became quite evident that *a national system of 'RANSC-style' records of achievement was not to be introduced and supported by regulations.* The reason for this was, I believe, simply that the political agenda had changed.

Shortly after the establishment of the records of achievement pilot schemes and the national evaluation, Sir Keith Joseph was replaced as Secretary of State by Kenneth Baker. Unlike his predecessor, Kenneth Baker was less concerned with single issues, such as the achievements of the less able, and more concerned with root and branch reform of the whole education service. Thus records of achievement ceased to be a priority as far as ministers were concerned. This allowed the pilot schemes, PRAISE and RANSC to get on with their work relatively undisturbed but it always held the possibility that, at the point when policy decisions had to be made, records of achievement would be accommodated to newer initiatives or be lost altogether.

In July 1987, as PRAISE was about to publish an interim report, the DES published its consultation document on a proposed National Curriculum for 5 to 16 year olds. As a consequence the national evaluation team was asked to draw attention in its report to any issues arising for records of achievement. Subsequently, RANSC also offered evidence to the Task Group on Assessment and Testing (TGAT, 1988, Appendix I) and drew attention to common aims and possible tensions between Records of Achievement and National Curriculum Assessment. In particular, RANSC indicated that some of the most central principles and procedures of records of achievement could become a source of tension, namely:

— the emphasis on the involvement of pupils in assessment and recording;
— the emphasis on positive achievement;
— the emphasis on formative, developmental purposes rather than the accountability of schools and local authorities;
— the emphasis on the accreditation of recording processes;
— the emphasis on recording pupils' total achievements, including personal qualities and general skills, rather than over-emphasizing attainment in single subjects;
— the emphasis on continuous assessment and recording.

Given the level of awareness at the time, these tensions between records of achievement and proposed National Curriculum assessment arrangements did not receive *detailed* attention in either the PRAISE final report or the RANSC report although the persistence of these issues was mentioned in both. In fact PRAISE was, on this occasion, 'steered' to confine its remarks to what had been observed in pilot records of achievement schemes rather than to speculate over-much on the likely effects of the introduction of national assessments (which, it was now argued, was outside its brief). The content of the RANSC report, which confined itself to rather weak statements such as: 'Further consideration will need to be given to the role of records of achievement in relation to the national curriculum information requirements' (RANSC, 1988, p. 17), indicates that similar pressures were operating at this level also.

Strategically it may have been wise not to draw too much attention to ideological tensions at this stage because the student-centred philosophy, which underpinned many records of achievement schemes, no longer had any obvious supporters in the Government. Had RANSC been more explicit about the philosophical contradictions between the two initiatives, there was a strong possibility that records of achievement, as embodied in the early statement of DES policy and developed in pilot schemes, would simply be dropped. It was already clear that nothing was going to be allowed to stop the National Curriculum and assessment juggernaut that was now on the road and had so much riding on it politically. The best hope was that some system could be worked out that would meet the new demands of Government for a means of reporting National Curriculum assessments as well as fulfilling the original aspirations of records of achievement schemes.

Shortly after SEAC had offered the results of its consultations on the RANSC report to the DES, and before ministers had had a chance to make the expected announcement regarding regulations, the Cabinet reshuffle on 24 July 1989 installed John McGregor as the new Secretary of State for England. He then went on holiday and the task of making the announcement fell to Angela Rumbold, Junior Minister of Education for schools. On the grounds that the requirements of regulations should be kept to a minimum 'so that they do not add to the volume of work already undertaken by schools in recording and reporting pupils' achievements', Mrs Rumbold's announcement was, as half expected, solely concerned with proposed regulations for *annual reports* to parents concerning the progress of pupils on National Curriculum subjects in both primary and secondary schools. She did not *endorse* the whole of SEAC's advice and she appeared careful to avoid using the term 'records of achievement'; instead she used the phrase 'recording and reporting pupils' achievements' which had less specific connotations.

This change in emphasis did not go unnoticed by education professionals who interpreted Mrs Rumbold's statement to mean that records of achievement were being killed off. In response, many groups and individuals who felt that this was one government initiative (alongside teacher appraisal) that had won the support of the profession, fired off letters of protest to both the DES and the educational press. By all accounts ministers were surprised by these brickbats and decided to mollify the profession by commending records of achievement. When the Draft Orders were published for consultation on 5 January 1990, they still remained free of any reference to records of achievement and prescribed only a system of annual reports to parents on achievements within National Curriculum subjects. However, they were now accompanied by a draft circular which referred both to PRAISE (in a footnote) and to RANSC and 'applauded' records of achievement which, by recognizing positive achievement and seeking to bring schools' policies on assessment, recording and reporting into a coherent whole, were seen to be 'very much in the spirit of the National Curriculum' (paras 27–9).

At this time additional pressure appears to have been brought to bear on the DES from the direction of the Training Agency. In November 1989 the Confederation of British Industry had called for a 'skills revolution' in which records of achievement were seen to have a crucial role (CBI, 1989, paras 39–41). On 5 December 1989 the Training Agency responded to the CBI initiative by sending its own guidelines on the use of records of achievement within TVEI to all

Chief Education Officers in England and Wales, who were invited to consider them alongside the draft orders on reporting which were about to emerge from the DES. There were marked contrasts between the two sets of documents and, although the DES would probably have denied disharmony between itself and the Training Agency, any observer might have been forgiven for interpreting the sequence of events as a case of the DES being upstaged. The Training Agency guidelines were very much closer to the recommendations of RANSC than either the draft orders or the draft circular from the DES. Moreover, the influence of the Training Agency on the future development of records of achievement was likely to be substantial. By 1990 all local authorities were involved with TVEI and the idea of profiling and individual action planning was built into TVEI contracts. Therefore, the Training Agency was in a position to insist on 'RANSC-style' records of achievement for all 14–18-year-olds involved with TVEI. Although the Training Agency was eventually disbanded, responsibility for TVEI continued within the new Training, Enterprise and Education Division of the Department of Employment.

Undoubtedly, the DES became aware that observers were interpreting these events as evidence that two government departments were pulling in different directions. Thus it became concerned to present a united front at the point when regulations on reporting were finally published. Significantly, on 10 July 1990 when the statutory instrument (no. 1381) was issued with Circular (8/90) entitled 'Records of Achievement', the Training Agency also issued its own 'Guidance for those managing TVEI', with respect to recording achievement.

Despite appearances, the final orders had not changed a great deal from the draft order stage. The regulations prescribed only the *minimum* requirements for annual reports to parents on individual pupil's achievements. At the ends of Key Stages these entailed reporting the results of statutory assessments by profile component and National Curriculum subject in terms of the level (1–10) achieved. In addition, parents were given the right to request information on achievement in the separate attainment targets. In the intervening years, when there is no statutory assessment, schools were required to give a written report on achievement in foundation subjects, although how this is done is a matter for discretion provided that it is made clear that any pupil scores given are not based on 'statutory arrangements' for assessments. In all years, schools were also expected to provide 'brief particulars' of achievement in other subjects and activities and the results of any public examination taken.

Within the accompanying Circular (8/90) the DES went somewhat further by endorsing the principles of records of achievement, as set out in the RANSC report, and commending the practice of fuller reporting on achievement. The Secretary of State for Education also joined with the Secretary of State for Employment in commending the guidelines for those working with the 14–18 age group in the context of TVEI. These set down principles intended to promote consistency in recording achievement and to establish a common format for documentation.

While the Government had moved back to a position of more overt support for records of achievement, its endorsement of principles, commendation of practice and applause for developments fell a long way short of the introduction of a national framework for records of achievement, supported by appropriate forms of validation or accreditation which were, in 1984, thought to be so essential for securing credibility. What we had, then, was a case of selective attention by the Government to evidence and advice, which it solicited, in order to fit policy to a new and different political agenda.

Undoubtedly, anxiety about the increased workload for schools without increased resources was a major issue. So too were the legal difficulties which would surround the introduction of a full-blown national system of records of achievement. (DES officials said that their legal department threw up their hands in horror at the thought of legislating for processes.) However, the DES must have been aware of the legal issues before it published its policy statement in 1984; how else could it have been made public and used as a basis for extensive pilot work supported by public funds? The education profession was not unaware of these difficulties but, for many, the principles of records of achievement, such as pupil involvement and broad-based positive recording, were fundamental and the feeling was that there should be no turning back. It seems therefore that the most serious challenge to Conservative Government policy (*circa* 1984) was from the Conservative Government of 1990.

Soon there were already indications that, in the absence of clear proposals for a national scheme, some schools and LEAs were pulling back from development. Elsewhere, where commitment was high, the dominant view was that National Curriculum reporting requirements could, and would be accommodated within the broader and more 'educational' conception of appropriate assessment, recording and reporting processes which records of achievement provided. If records of achievement were to survive, it now seemed unlikely to be as a result of government policy but because they returned to the grass-roots from whence they came. But this was not quite the end of the story. Towards the end of 1990 the Education Secretary announced that a proposed core format for a National Record of Achievement (NRA) would be sent out for limited consultation. This happened on 5 December and by February 1991 the National Record of Achievement had been formally launched by the DES and the Employment Department with the expectation that it would be used by schools with school leavers in the summer of 1991.

This train of events could lead one to assume that PRAISE, through RANSC, had been influential in the policy-making process after all. However, the NRA was principally the brain child of the Employment Department, not the DES, and the emphasis was on building up a life long record from age 16. The stated aims of the NRA indicated direct descent from the 1984 DES policy statement (compare the following with those quoted earlier in this chapter).

- to recognise and value the individual's learning and achievement
- to motivate the learner and support continuing development
- to act as a summary record for use with third parties
- to support the management of learner centred delivery.

But the way that these aims were to be put into practice received little attention at this time. To all intents and purposes the NRA was an artifact: a set of documents in a plastic, burgundy-coloured, gilt-edged folder which rapidly became known as the 'wine list'. All the advice contained in the PRAISE and RANSC reports concerning recording processes and the need for a system of quality assurance to give the document credibility seemed to have been ignored. Even the very practical point that school leavers in July need to complete their records by the preceding January or February, if they are to be used in applications to colleges or prospective employers, seemed to have been overlooked at the NRA launch. Understandably, early take-up of the NRA was patchy, although there was considerable incentive in that it was offered free to schools.

After responsibility for the NRA was handed over to the National Council for Vocational Qualifications (NCVQ) in April 1992, attention turned to incorporating action planning, to revising the document to give less of a 'school-feel' and to developing a model for quality assurance. At the time of writing, the results of this NRA development programme are yet to be revealed. For many of those who were closely involved in the DES pilots and PRAISE there is a sense of *deja vu* and a strong urge to ask whether the government had learned anything from the £10m of public funds spent on piloting and evaluation in the 1980s.

The evidence suggests that if RANSC, and by implication PRAISE, had an influence, it was less on policy-making within the DES than on thinking, policy and practice within schools, LEAs, and TVEI projects. As someone said to me, 'PRAISE informed the *Zeitgeist*' and we need to acknowledge that this may, in the long run, be as important as having the direct impact on government policy-making that we were led to expect. Interestingly, in a paper produced for colleagues in TEED, Macintosh (1992) made the point that: 'As far as schools are concerned it is likely that NCVQ will go back to RANSC whose recommentations are of course squarely in tune with current best practice in schools' (p. 16). So PRAISE may have an impact on policy making after all, but in a very indirect and delayed way that contradicts received wisdom on the role of evaluation.

## An Evaluation of the Evaluation

So what judgment of the ultimate value of the national evaluation of records of achievement does all this lead to? One judgment would be that despite its considerable achievement in informing RANSC, PRAISE has simply shared the fate of many other evaluations. The weight of evidence gathered in independent inquiry has rarely been able to influence the ultimate shape of policy in the face of strong political imperative; therefore we have to countenance the possibility that the PRAISE report (and even the RANSC report) was consigned to the filing cabinet as far as our sponsor (the DES) was concerned. If this was the case then the other audiences for our report — LEAs, schools and, indeed, bodies such as the Employment Department — may emerge as more important, as we probably suspected all along. In that legislation does not *proscribe* learner-centred RANSC-style records of achievement, then it is likely that a good proportion of schools and LEAs have drawn on the information in the PRAISE and RANSC reports when making decisions about their assessment, recording and reporting systems. In other words there are decision-makers, other than those at the DES, who have made use of the RANSC report and the PRAISE evaluation.

A desire to provide information for these other audiences was, in fact, a main motivation for including detailed illustrations of practice in the PRAISE report and for publishing detailed whole-school case-studies. We knew that much of this kind of information would be of limited interest to the DES, or even RANSC, but we thought it would provide schools and LEAs with some answers to their questions about what records of achievement systems might look like in particular contexts. Of course, this additional use of the PRAISE evaluation was only made possible because we were able to make public our findings.

For a number of reasons PRAISE enjoyed a generally good relationship with DES officials. One reason was undoubtedly to do with the
relative lack of political sensitivity concerning the records of achievement initiative in its initial stages; another reason was to do with the
channels of regular communication maintained between members of
the team and the DES which resulted in very practical assistance in the
printing and distribution of reports.

We were well aware that we could not take for granted this kind
of support in disseminating our findings beyond the DES and RANSC.
As is now common in government-funded research, we had received
a contract which gave the DES the power to impose certain restrictions
on the conduct of the inquiry, to claim ownership of the data and to
limit our freedom to publish and disseminate findings. We had secured
agreement that the DES should not unreasonably withold publication,
and, at the first meeting of the evaluation sub-committee of RANSC,
we had tabled a set of ethical guidelines for the conduct of the research
which stated that we should not expect to release data or reports without first negotiating clearance with participants. However, had the
DES wished to exercise its power to impose restrictions, the status of
PRAISE as an independent evaluation, and our desire to communicate
our findings to other audiences, would clearly have been put in jeopardy.

For the reasons already mentioned, PRAISE emerged relatively
unscathed; none of our reports, or substantial sections of our reports,
was suppressed by our sponsor. This is not to say that publication was
entirely plain sailing. We encountered a few situations where we were
under pressure, usually from senior management of schools or pilot
schemes, but sometimes from the DES, to amend or abandon reports.
We had anticipated this kind of situation, hence the ethical guidelines
which, for example, made provision for a dialogue to validate and
'clear' findings with participants. These procedures also allowed them
a right of reply if, in the last analysis, our interpretation of the evidence
still differed from theirs. Although negotiation over clearance proved
to be a very lengthy process, it ensured that detailed accounts of records
of achievement policy and practice, at all levels, became publicly
available at various points in the life of the project (a kind of controlled
'leaking'). It also, I think, strengthened our accounts by helping us to
ensure that we represented the range of perspectives and value-positions
taken in relation to the initiative. Although there were areas in which
we undoubtedly fell short, we felt that we had done as much as we
were able to do to fulfil MacDonald's (1977) aspiration for democratic
evaluation that it should provide an 'information service to the community about the characteristics of an educational programme'.

## Implications

The lesson which can be drawn from this experience is quite simple and probably 'what everybody knows' anyway. The power of research-based evaluation to provide evidence on which rational decisions can be expected to be made is quite limited. Policy-makers will always find reasons to ignore, or be highly selective of, evaluation findings if the information does not support the particular political agenda operating at the time when decisions have to be made.

Given this reality, the best that evaluators can do is to try to ensure that their accounts are made public so that the 'citizenry', and especially those whose lives or practice will be affected by policy decisions, have the kind of information which will enable them to make considered judgments about the wisdom of decisions taken on their behalf. This aspiration therefore defines the essential role of evaluation as supportive of the democratic ideal.

Of course, at a time when increasing restrictions are being placed on funded research, especially government-funded research, it is not always easy to ensure that research-based evaluation reports pass into the public domain. There are limits to what can be achieved by diplomacy, although I think this was a fairly successful aspect of the strategy adopted by PRAISE. Moreover, the extent to which each project can be expected to work out its own salvation is also limited.

In March 1988, a British Educational Research Association (BERA) seminar was convened in Cambridge to consider issues concerning contractual arrangements between researchers and sponsors and to begin to develop a code of practice for funded educational research. The provisional code that emerged from these deliberations addressed the issues concerning publication — which have been a main theme in this chapter — and recommended that research proposals should have reference to:

— The principle that researcher(s) have a duty to report to the sponsor and to the wider public, including educational 'practitioners' and other interested parties. The right to publish is therefore entailed by this duty to report.
— The right to publish is essential to the long-term viability of the research activity, to the credibility of the researcher (and of the sponsor when it seeks to use research finding in its support) and to the interest of an open society (Elliott, 1989, p. 16).

This provisional code of practice also considered the conditions under which the right to publish might be legitimately restricted, the right of researchers to dissociate themselves from misleadingly selective accounts of the research, and the principle of dissemination as an integral and ongoing part of the research process (not simply as a final act which can fall victim to suppression).

Members of the BERA seminar were also aware of the need for a collective effort on the part of educational researchers and research institutions in order to encourage support for such a code of practice and to put pressure on sponsors to accept it. For this reason a number of recommendations were made to BERA to engage in dialogue with other relevant agencies, including research sponsors, to promote the adoption of a code of practice and to support arguments against restrictive sponsor control of educational research.

One cannot be entirely sanguine about the likely outcome of such moves, even if they receive widespread support in principle, because research sponsors hold most of the important cards — notably the money in which resides the power. Little can now be achieved in research terms without sponsorship, and even funds for non-sponsored research will be received by universities in proportion to judgments of their research output and their ability to attract sponsorship. Thus researchers have been put in the market-place and are expected to compete against one another for scarce resources.

The strategy of divide-and-rule is not conducive to collective effort in support of academic freedom and the principle of intellectual integrity in a free society. Instead it encourages unreasonable cost-cutting and compliance in order to secure scarce research contracts — and often the jobs of the insecure workforce of contract researchers. Thus, those who would wish to promote an agreed code of practice for educational research and evaluation are not exactly arguing from a position of great strength. However, since one cannot expect to win the war without doing battle, it must be worth working to create a climate of opinion, and a critical mass of support, that will reaffirm the values underpinning the pursuit of truth in a democratic and open society. Unless this happens, most research-based evaluation on policy issues will almost inevitably become a bureaucratic device for rationalizing policy decisions already made or in the offing: 'an unconditional service to those government agencies which have major control over the allocation of educational resources', lacking independence and having no control over the use made of information (MacDonald, 1977, p. 226).

If, however, we are able to ensure that the information gets out and, as with PRAISE, has some opportunity to inform the *Zeitgeist* then we can take some satisfaction from the knowledge that knowledge itself cannot be unknown. Once in the public domain it has the possibility of influencing both practice and policy although the decision-makers might be other than those to whom the evaluation was supposed, initially, to be addressed.

### Notes

1  The views expressed in this chapter are the author's own opinions and should not be taken to represent the views of the PRAISE team or the DES/WO.
2  Those who are interested might like to compare, for instance, the following sections of the two reports:

| RANSC Report, 1989 | | PRAISE Report, 1988 | |
|---|---|---|---|
| para. | 3.22 | page | 29–30 |
| | 3.25 | | 3–4 |
| | 3.43 | | 6 |
| | 3.55 | | 61 |
| | 3.64 | | 59 |
| | 3.66 | | 58 |
| | 3.71 | | 51 |
| | 4.2 | | 6 |
| | 4.3 | | 8 |
| | 4.4 | | 11 |
| | 4.5 | | 26 |
| | 4.10 | | 23–26 |
| | 4.25 | | 92 |
| | 5.19 | | 109–110 |

### References

BROWN, S. and BLACK, H. (1988) 'Profiles and Records of Achievement' in BROWN, S. (Ed.) *Assessment: A Changing Practice*, Edinburgh, Scottish Academic Press.

CBI (1989) *Towards a Skills Revolution: Report of the Vocational Education and Training Task Force*, London, CBI.

CRONBACH, L. (1963) 'Course Improvement through Evaluation', *Teachers' College Record*, **64**, pp. 672–83.

DAVIS, E. (1981) *Teachers as Curriculum Evaluators*, London, Allen and Unwin.

DES (1984) *Records of Achievement: A Statement of Policy*.

ELLIOTT, J. (1989) 'Towards a Code of Practice for Funded Educational Research', *Research Intelligence*, February, pp. 14–18.

FAIRBAIRN, D. (1988) 'Pupil Profiling: New Approaches to Recording and Reporting Achievement', in MURPHY, R. and TORRANCE, H. (Eds) *The*

*Changing Face of Educational Assessment*, Milton Keynes, Open University Press.

MacIntosh, H. (1992) *Update on Current Assessment and Accreditation Issues*, (mimeograph 25 March).

MacDonald, B. (1977) 'A Political Classification of Evaluation Studies', in Hamilton, D. *et al.* (Eds) *Beyond the Numbers Game*, London, Macmillan.

Newsom, J. (1963) *Half Our Future*, London, HMSO.

Norwood, C. (1943) *Curriculum and Examinations in Secondary Schools*, London, HMSO.

PRAISE (Broadfoot, P., James, M., McMeeking, S., Nuttall, D. and Stierer, B.) (1988) *Records of Achievement: Report of the National Evaluation of Pilot Schemes*, London, HMSO.

RANSC (1988) *Records of Achievement: Report of the Records of Achievement National Steering Committee*, London, DES/WO.

Simons, H. (1987) *Getting to Know Schools in a Democracy: The Politics and Process of Evaluation*, London, Falmer Press.

Spens, W. (1938) *Report on Consultative Committee on Secondary Education with Special Reference to Grammar Schools and Technical High Schools*, London, HMSO.

Stufflebeam, D. *et al.* (1971) *Educational Evaluation and Decision-making*, Itasca, IL, F.E. Peacock for Phi Delta Kappon Study Committee on Evaluation.

TGAT (1988) *National Curriculum: Task Group on Assessment and Testing: A Report*, London, DES/WO.

# 9    Changing Times, Changing Identities: Grieving for a Lost Self

*Jennifer Nias*

This chapter arises out of research which I have undertaken in the past fifteen years into the lives and careers of primary teachers. It is however an extension of the thinking behind that research, born of close contact with the teaching profession through my present job — that of in-service education with experienced teachers — as I and they have faced the tensions and changes of the past few years. In the first part, I argue that teaching, especially in primary schools, calls for a heavy investment of the self in work. I then suggest that teachers have been subject, in the past few years, to such radical social, economic and legislative changes that many feel bereaved, in that they have lost the key relationships which gave meaning and purpose to their professional lives, and therefore to their self-conceptions. Their response has been to grieve, an inherently conflictual process in which the bereaved swings emotionally between a desire to cling on to and to deny the past. Finally I indicate ways in which policy and practice might be adapted to help teachers through the lengthy ordeal of grieving for their lost selves and towards the construction of new identities.

The research itself is fully reported in Nias (1989). As the title of that book suggested, on two occasions between 1974 and 1985, I listened extensively to the same practitioners talking about how they experienced teaching as work. The first time, between 1974 and 1976, the ninety-nine teachers whom I interviewed had been in the profession for a period of between two and nine years or had recently left it. On the second occasion, in 1985, I spoke to about half this number. Most had been teaching for between nine and eighteen years or were taking up careers again after a period of child-raising. Throughout, the proportion of women to men was about three to one. Full details of the methodology used for data collection and analysis are given in Nias (1989; 1992). Briefly, I used semi-structured interviews of which, in 1974–76, I took shorthand notes or which, in 1985, were tape-recorded and transcribed so that my interviewees had the opportunity to see and verify what they had said. Interviews took place anywhere that was convenient to individuals and were conducted in their homes or schools, in restaurants, pubs or, on a few occasions, over the telephone. Typically, they were long, the shortest being forty-five minutes and the longest five hours. Most lasted about one and a half hours. My role was chiefly that of listener, though I also asked probe questions and occasionally encouraged the interview to become a conversation. My concern throughout was to try to understand how teachers themselves experienced the job of teaching and where it fitted into their lives and concerns.

My analysis of the data was slow and intermittent, for reasons that I have explained in Nias (1992). The benefit of this was that it enabled me fully to appreciate the predominant characteristic of primary teachers' relationship with their work. Over and over again, at all stages of their careers, I was presented with evidence of their professional self-referentialism. This is not to suggest high levels of individual or occupational egocentricity, but rather to argue that teachers appear to construe the purpose and meaning of their work in terms of its impact upon the self. Lacking any evidence as to whether or not this is always the case in the professions or semi-professions, I looked further into primary teaching itself to see if there was anything about it which would explain the particular way in which my interviewees talked about their experience, their standards, their past, present and future careers, their relationships with pupils and colleagues. I concluded that, as work, primary teaching makes very heavy demands upon the person who becomes the teacher. Tradition, teacher education, experience and conventional wisdom continually emphasize the uniqueness of the individual, the specificity of context and the primacy of the person.

There are several reasons why this should be the case, most of them arising from occupational traditions. One, however, is rooted in the perceptual basis of teaching. Minute by minute, within the shifting, unpredictable, capricious world of the classroom, teachers have to make decisions and reach judgments. What they 'see' and do therefore depends upon their unique perceptions of specific events, behaviours, materials and persons. In turn, these perceptions are rooted in 'basic assumptions' (Abercrombie, 1969) which are slowly built up, extended and modified as, from birth, we develop and exercise the skills of seeing (or hearing, smelling, tasting, touching) and as we experience the emotions which accompany these activities. Since no two people have the same life experiences, we all learn to perceive the world and ourselves as part of it in different ways. So teachers, as people, 'see' and interpret their pupils and the latter's actions and reactions according to perceptual patterns which are unique to themselves. No matter how pervasive particular aspects of a shared social or occupational culture may be or how well individuals are socialized into it, the attitudes and actions of all teachers are rooted in their own ways of perceiving the world. In this sense, teaching cannot be otherwise than personal.

Yet the reasons for professional individualism are also profoundly cultural. In the first place, teaching is often a private activity. Until recently, the architectural design of most English primary schools has unquestioningly followed the tradition, established in urban elementary schools in the nineteenth century, that instruction is best carried out in 'box' classrooms occupied by one teacher and a group of thirty to forty children. These classrooms are usually cut off from one another and windows may be placed so that it is difficult for passing teachers to see into one another's rooms. Furthermore, few primary schools allow teachers non-contact time in which to talk or work together; breaks are short and in any case, the pressures of class teaching dictate that many teachers spend a large proportion of their breaks in the classroom itself. The isolation imposed upon them in these ways has helped to foster an occupational context from which they learn to expect that much of their working lives will be spent with children, not adults; teaching will be not only personal but solitary, even lonely.

Loneliness is compounded by the perceived need to be self-reliant. Many of my interviewees recalled feeling very unsupported in their early months or years in the job because they believed either that there was no one with time or relevant experience to whom they could turn or that to admit to classroom difficulties was to be labelled as a pedagogical failure. That the latter tradition persists is apparent from recent research projects into adult relationships in school (Nias *et al.*, 1989; Nias *et al.*, 1992). During the fieldwork for these projects, we worked in staff groups whose members freely and habitually supported and worked with one another in and outside the classroom. The ways in which they did so pointed up the relative infrequency with which such collaboration occurs. Moreover, we found that teachers who have formed in their earlier professional experience the habit of institutionalized self-reliance tend to carry this expectation with them to other schools, with the result that they sometimes fail to perceive the help which is available in their new environments. Further, initial teacher education provides students with relatively few chances to observe their more experienced colleagues in action and, except in open-plan schools, the latter seldom see one another teaching. This lack of opportunity to 'sit by Nellie' encourages students and probationers to feel that they must survive by their own efforts and to believe in an occupational *rite de passage* which equates the establishment of competence with suffering. As many have argued (notably Lortie, 1975, and Hargreaves, 1980), teachers have little opportunity or incentive to develop shared professional knowledge or a collegial sense of the 'state of the art'.

These autonomous tendencies have been encouraged by the relative freedom from political control which primary teachers have until recently taken for granted. For much of the past hundred years, teachers in Britain have felt that it was their responsibility to make far-reaching decisions about the curriculum and teaching methods used in their classes, to the point, as HMI have continually reminded us in the past decade, that there is often little curriculum continuity from class to class and sometimes little communication between teachers who have frequently learnt to depend upon their own knowledge, interests and preferences in making pedagogical and curricular decisions. Indeed, this freedom from external constraints and collegial influence has been for some teachers one of the main attractions of the job. Many are apprehensive about the introduction of the National Curriculum not so much because they disagree with its content but because they fear that it will limit their ability to use their unique talents and expertise for the benefit of the children whom they teach (Nias *et al.*, 1992).

Traditionally, primary teachers have also tended to enjoy a considerable degree of ideological freedom. This is particularly important to many of them because of a deep commitment to their own religious, moral, political or social values. The pluralism and epistemological confusion to which many recent accounts (for example, Alexander, 1984; Delamont, 1987) of primary schooling have drawn attention, allow those teachers and headteachers who have a coherent philosophy to pursue it with relative impunity. Despite recent political developments, the English system still offers plenty of scope to individuals who wish to propagate particular values or views of the educational process.

Primary teachers' readiness to rely upon their own knowledge, skills, personality and values is further encouraged by their allegiance to philosophical traditions which see the personal relationship between teacher and learner as central to the educational process. Onto the Romantic preoccupation with the individual exemplified by Rousseau's *Emile*, practising educationalists in the nineteenth century grafted the Christian tradition, expressed by Froebel and Pestalozzi as respect and concern for the whole child and by Buber and Rogers as the 'I-Thou' relationship (in which the teacher as a person becomes a resource for the self-activated development of the learner). Today many primary school teachers still see the personal relationship which they have with individual children not just as a means of establishing control and increasing motivation but also as the means by which education itself takes place.

Moreover, throughout their professional education and socialization, teachers are led to believe that they are capable of 'knowing' not just one child, but all the pupils in their care (Alexander, 1984). One of the first teacher training colleges in England (St John's, Battersea) was informed by Pestalozzi's belief that teaching was an expression of love and that teachers should therefore live and work among their pupils. This aspiration was itself drawn partially from Froebel's metaphysical concern for the centrality of unity and wholeness and his consequent belief that education should be an organic process, free from artificial and damaging divisions. Teachers socialized into this tradition, as many primary teachers are, tend to identify with their classes, to talk of themselves in relationship to their pupils as 'we'. They tacitly believe that their personal relationship is with the whole class, not just one child.

Teaching has a further set of characteristics which encourages the investment of self in work. It is very 'inclusive' (Argyris, 1964), that is, it absorbs much time and energy and makes use of many of the individual's talents, skills or abilities. Practitioners who allow or encourage their jobs to be 'inclusive' find that teaching is personal in a double sense: it draws upon interests and capacities which might in other occupations be reserved for non-work activities and it allows little space for the development of alternative lives. In particular, the more demanding it becomes of imagination, insight, problem-solving and professional skills, the more it offers an outlet for creative potential, thereby reducing individuals' needs to seek this elsewhere. Similarly, when teaching is conceptualized as a relationship between two or more people, rather than as an instrumental activity, it becomes possible for teachers to find personal and emotional satisfactions within their working lives rather than to look for them in other places.

The fact that teaching as an occupation is potentially 'inclusive' is compounded by the chronic scarcity of resources from which it suffers. By definition, no teacher ever has enough time, energy and material resources to meet all the learning and personal demands of a large class of young children. To this shortage are now added expenditure cuts at both local and national levels. Yet as an occupation, teaching has a bottomless appetite for 'commitment' ('a readiness to allocate scarce personal resources', Lortie, 1975, p. 189). As a result, teachers are easily trapped. The more they identify with their jobs, the greater the satisfaction they receive from their personal relationship with individuals and classes. Similarly, the more outlet they find in their work for varied talents and abilities, the greater the incentive for them to invest their own personal and material resources in their teaching. They become the victims of a double paradox: the personal rewards to be found in their work come only from self-investment in it, yet when the cost of the latter is too high to be paid, its rewards are also reduced.

All this adds up to a persistent historical tradition in many English-speaking countries which emphasizes the importance of the individual teacher's personality (Lortie, 1975; Woods, 1981; Connell, 1985; Pollard, 1985; Sikes et al., 1985; Nias, 1989). This tradition is not confined to practitioners. The Department of Education and Science have argued: 'HMI found that the personal qualities of the teachers were in many cases the decisive factor in their effectiveness. A similar view was put forward by schools' (DES, 1982, para. 6.2), and: 'Personality, character and commitment are as important as the specific knowledge and skills that are used in the day to day tasks of teaching' (DES, 1983, para. 1.26).

Furthermore, schools, as organizations, often seem to discourage the development not just of shared professional knowledge but also of a common vocabulary with agreed meanings. A vicious circle exists. Class teachers have little time, opportunity, incentive or reason for professional interaction or discussion. They therefore continue to attach idiosyncratic meanings to words and concepts, so creating two further obstacles to interaction: they fail to reach agreement and lose the desire to go on meeting or they agree at the level of words alone. In the latter case, because consensus is based upon individual ideas which have not been modified through contact with others' perspectives, it soon breaks down, deepening practitioners' sense that they have little to gain from talking to one another.

That primary teachers in England are often reluctant to engage in a genuine exchange of views on educational issues, especially within their own schools, may also derive in part from the nature of the training they receive. Historically, teacher education has lacked a tradition of debating philosophical differences or educational priorities, when to do this would lead to intellectual conflict (a situation which may in the past have been exacerbated by the small size of many colleges). The unity, naturalism and pragmatism of Froebel and Dewey have been more influential than the dialecticism of Hegel and Marx in shaping the professional education of most primary and many secondary teachers. Furthermore teachers are generally trained to work with children in classrooms, not with adults in schools. They are given little understanding of schools as institutions or preparation for negotiation or conflict resolution among their colleagues. When differences occur they are often resolved, at least on the surface, by reference to authority. As a result, few structures exist within schools to deal with the disagreements which inevitably occur in an individualistic profession. Moreover, in primary schools in particular, the pervasive existence of 'good relationships' as an unchallenged educational aim often results in the proscription of negative emotions (such as anger and jealousy) among adults as well as among children. For all these reasons, potential conflict in school staff-rooms tends to be treated as a pathological symptom rather than as a naturally occuring phenomenon, the resolution of which can lead to personal and collective growth and to the development of shared meanings and understandings.

It is not surprising then that the teachers to whom I spoke should have been persistently self-referential. The tradition and nature of their work impelled them towards self-investment in it, their senses of personal and of professional identity were closely entwined. No matter how tenuous or short-term their commitment to teaching as a career, as work it deeply involved the individual persons whom they saw themselves to be. The investment was even greater for those people who had reached a point in their professional development when they took on the identity of 'teacher', that is, when they 'became' teachers, rather than simply doing the job (see Nias, 1989, for an elaboration of this point) than for those who had not yet made this identification. But it existed in some measure for them all.

Three consequences ensued. First, no matter what their stage of professional development, individual teachers' sense of personal worth, or self-esteem, was very dependent on circumstances and events in their professional lives. Second, the preservation of self-image, the protection of a core of self-defining values became a matter of enduring professional concern (Woods, 1981; Pollard, 1985; Nias, 1989). Third, established practitioners (that is, those who had come to see themselves as 'teachers') imbued their relationships with their pupils, colleagues, parents or other persons with whom they came into close professional contact, with a sense of self-defining meaning and purpose. Radical changes in these relationships threatened the individual teacher's very sense of personal identity.

For the rest of this chapter, I am concerned with the impact of recent changes upon the last two aspects of primary teachers' self-investment in work. This is not to suggest that the potential impact of such change upon their sense of self-esteem is unimportant. However, it is variable. Not only do individuals differ in their tolerance for ambiguity and their readiness to see opportunities for self-extension in new circumstances, but also external change has a greater or lesser impact upon different types of educational work at different times (for example, in schools, the introduction of the National Curriculum has greatly enhanced the professional importance of those with expertise in technology, while reducing the perceived need for music specialists).

In considering teachers' reactions to recent changes in terms of their self-conceptions, I have adopted the theoretical perspective of symbolic interactionism, for reasons which I have detailed in Nias (1989). This sociological tradition makes a distinction between the self as 'I' — rebellious, creative, autonomous, hard to define and, I have suggested, largely ignored in educational literature — and the self as 'me' — the accumulated product of early social conditioning by 'significant others' supported in later life by 'reference groups'. In relation to the self as 'me' I have also adopted the distinction made by some authors between 'situational selves' which vary with context, and the 'substantial self', a deeply protected core of self-defining beliefs, assumptions and values which, though in the first instance acquired through social conditioning, becomes so much part of the individual's sense of personal identity that it varies very little with circumstances.

The substantial self is particularly difficult to change, because it is rooted in the conscious or unconscious past and in those relationships which helped to shape it. The assumptions which it incorporates are deeply embedded and, because many of them 'were established before the child could talk, and, having been made non-verbally, are very difficult to talk about' (Abercrombie, 1969, p. 73), individuals may find it hard to discover what their beliefs and values are or to lay them out to challenge from others. Moreover, the fact that many basic assumptions are formed, especially at home and at school, in situations where children are physically, emotionally or intellectually dependent upon those who are tending or teaching them, often means that a perceived need to change is tacitly linked in an individual's mind with a challenge to authority. The less ready individuals are, through temperament or training, to make this challenge, the more they will resist perceiving the evidence which would result in accommodation to new ideas. Authority-dependence may be closely linked with a reluctance to surrender the past or to modify the self-image through the incorporation of new ideas (Abercrombie, 1969).

Perceived threats to the substantial self are likely then to be opposed or rejected. To the extent that change is imposed on individuals from outside them, it will also be accompanied by a sense of losing control. Teachers are particularly vulnerable in this respect because of the occupational importance which is attached to 'being in control'. Many studies of teachers have drawn attention to the fact that they think they are judged (by pupils, parents, superiors, peers) in terms of their ability to maintain discipline and that they do not feel themselves to have attained a full professional identity until they are 'in control'. The sense of powerlessness which attends any enforced change in self-image is thus aggravated for teachers by the fear that their ability as practitioners is being called in question.

For all these reasons, individual teachers are unlikely easily to change the way they see themselves and will stubbornly protect the professional relationships which protect their sense of identity. Yet many have been unable in the past few years to prevent radical alterations to their occupational relationships. Their sense of moral accountability to individual pupils, and through them to parents, has been threatened by the introduction into schooling of devolved budgets, market economics, the threat of narrowly-defined outcome assessments and the introduction of league tables of results. Their capacity to fulfil their professional obligations to the standard they expect of themselves has been undermined by rising class numbers, poor buildings, equipment and facilities, reductions in resource levels, a shortage of skilled personnel and an overcrowded National Curriculum. Constant attacks from central government, the media and, occasionally, parents or governors has sometimes given them the sense that their commitment is in doubt, that they are no longer trusted to do their best for the children for whom they often care very deeply and for whose well-being and progress they feel personally responsible. Changes equally radical in scope and intention have affected advisers, inspectors, education officers and members of HMI, and are threatening the stability of teacher educators.

It is no exaggeration to describe the impact of such changes upon many members of the education service and, in the context of this chapter, upon primary teachers in particular, in the terms which Marris (1986, p. x) uses for bereavement, that is as a change so fundamental that it disrupts 'our ability to organise experience in a meaningful way'. At the centre of Marris' argument (presented in 1958 and 1986) is his claim that 'the fundamental crisis of bereavement arises not from the loss of others, but from the loss of self' (1986, p. 33). So, when the central professional relationships of educationists' lives are disrupted, they lose a crucial part of their identities. The greater their self-investment in work, the more this is the case, for as Marris states

> our purposes and expectations come to be organised about particular relationships which are then crucial to the way we constitute the meaning of our lives. When we lose such a relationship, the whole structure of meaning centred upon it disintegrates. The intense anxiety, restlessness and despair which bereavement characteristically provokes express the profound threat which this presents (1986, p. vii).

It is an important part of Marris' argument that this sense of utter disorientation can be occasioned not just by bereavement in its accepted sense, but also by the disruption of other social relationships which give purpose and meaning to people's lives. So, for example, redundancy or enforced retirement, physical dislocation such as that experienced by refugees or people resettled into new housing areas, rapid change from one form of social or economic structure to another can be experienced as a bereavement just as painful and disequilibrating as that occasioned by, for example, death, divorce or enforced separation. What all these changes have in common is a disintegration of individual meaning, as this was constructed by and invested in purposive relationships.

It does not matter that these relationships do not seem to others (for example, in the case of teachers to pupils, parents, politicians) as they do to the bereaved themselves, since it is individuals' own definition of meaning which has salience for them. Social changes which disrupt the patterns of relationship upon which individuals or groups depend will threaten their ability to experience life as meaningful, no matter how rational these changes may seem from the point of view of others with different relationships and therefore with a different sense of purpose.

Moreover, resistance to change which appears to threaten self-defining relationships should not be seen as irrational behaviour or pusillanimity. Rather, the 'conservative impulse' (Marris, 1986, p. 5) is necessary to life, for, as Abercrombie (1969) also points out, without regularity we could not make sense of what is happening around us nor predict what is likely to happen next. We must attempt to defend the validity of what we have learnt, to preserve some continuity between past and present, because if we did not we should be helpless, driven back as adults to the learning state of infants. Indeed as Bettelheim (1961) and Goffman (1968) have so vividly described, one of the first tasks of 'total' institutions such as prisons and mental hospitals is to deprive newcomers of their established structures of meaning, in order to socialize them into a fresh environment with different principles of order and relevance.

However tenaciously we defend our established perceptual frameworks, circumstances sometimes force us into situations in which we cannot sustain any continuity of meaning, because the relationships which embodied that meaning have radically changed or have disappeared. Yet our wish to retain the reasons for caring, working or living which were represented by those relationships remains. Accordingly, we swing between conflicting desires: to cling on to that which is lost and so to maintain established meanings, and to escape from it, in order to construct new meanings which will give life renewed purpose. Grief is the expression of these irreconcilable urges, of a 'profound conflict between contradictory impulses' (Marris, 1986, p. 31). Mourning is the process which facilitates the articulation of this conflict, by imposing socially-approved stages upon its resolution.

During the process of grieving, individuals try to regain control over that part of their lives which has been rendered unmanageable by a loss of meaning. They do this by gradually restoring predictability to it, that is, by imposing fresh meanings upon the world about them. However, such meanings must contain some continuity with the past, unless all attempt to live in an ordered world is to be abandoned. The resolution of grief can therefore be seen as a process of abstracting 'the essential meaning of the past and reinterpreting it to fit a very different future' (Marris, 1986, p. 34). To recover from bereavement is to formulate a different sense of identity which integrates past, present and future within new relationships which contain some thread of continuity with the old. Familiar assumptions are not totally discredited; instead they are subsumed into fresh purposes which enable life to continue in ways which seem meaningful and, so, manageable.

However, grief is not always resolved. Sometimes people retreat from or in other ways deny their loss, clinging ineffectively, at times in a fantasy world, to a past which no longer exists. They may attempt to forget the past altogether, but such a denial of the experience upon which their sense of personal identity is built can lead to alienation, aimlessness, cynicism. They may refuse to give outward expression to their sense of loss, turning their conflict inward instead and in the process generating apathy, depression, tension, guilt, on the one hand or outbursts of violent anger on the other. Whichever path is followed, it impedes the resumption of a new life and locks up or directs into unproductive channels energy which is needed for the making of fresh meaning.

To view as bereavement the reaction of many members of the education service to recent changes helps us to explain their response to innovations which, it might be claimed, directly affect their working rather than their personal lives and from which they might therefore be expected to be reasonably detached. It also allows us to reconsider how we can help ourselves and others to adjust to enforced change. I wonder what our behaviour as policy-makers, administrators, inspectors, teachers, educational leaders or teacher educators might be, if we stopped talking about 'the management of change' or 'the management of stress' and spoke instead of 'helping to find a constructive resolution to bereavement' or 'helping the articulation of grief'. It is the latter path which I follow for the rest of this chapter, drawing on insights from social psychology and psychotherapy, rather than from the growing literature on educational management. I make four main points.

First, whatever our professional position we must recognize that bereavement is both threatening and inherently conflictual. It is threatening because it involves the loss of structures which give our lives meaning and so it carries with it the fear of disintegration. Lacking the ability to impose meaning, and so predictability, relevance and order, upon the world of perception, emotions and ideas that we inhabit, our sense of purpose too is menaced. Life becomes, for the moment, unmanageable. I have suggested that teachers find professional bereavement especially difficult because they are socialized into a personal respect and occupational need for control and are therefore very vulnerable to the threat of meaninglessness, with its implications of potential chaos. This crisis can be resolved by a reintegration of meaning in which neither the past nor the loss are denied, but, instead, meaning and purpose are reformulated in terms of the present and the future. However, 'the transformation of familiar assumptions about the world and one's place in it is profoundly disturbing' (Marris, 1986, p. 151). Accordingly, the sense of confusion and disquiet which follows bereavement can be accommodated and integrated into a new structure of purpose and meaning only through expression of the internal conflict that it represents. Such expression may be manifested in many ways, from violent emotional outbursts to the rule-governed articulation and negotiation of differences. What we must realize is that whatever form grief takes, it is an inevitable response to losses which cannot be readily assimilated, that it is necessarily attended by contradictory feelings and that the open expression of these emotions, many of them negative, is part of its resolution. At the simplest level, then we must recognize the threatening nature of change and of its resolution and

then make room in schools for the expression of the emotion it pro-
vokes. In particular, we should not proscribe, as many primary schools
tend to do, the voicing of anger, frustration, hostility, desolation, even
despair.

It may also be helpful deliberately to provide or promote opportunities for the individual or collective expression of ambivalent reactions to change. Many such opportunities already exist though they are
not always recognized as offering this potential. For example, appraisal
interviews, department, team or staff meetings, professional association meetings, in-service courses, are all in different ways occasions
when people can voice their feelings, can express their inner sense of
conflict, sometimes by projecting this upon a real or imagined foe, and
can search together for new identities, a fresh sense of professional
meaning and purpose.

There are also those who claim, as Marris does, that an organized
process of mourning helps the articulation of grief and makes it easier
to accept both the severance of a past relationship and the possible
preservation of its essential meaning into the future. The following
two examples are taken from the period soon after the 1988 Education
Act was passed. During 1988–89 I worked as a part-time teacher in a
primary school, as part of a research project into whole school curriculum development (Nias *et al.*, 1992). In that capacity I participated
in many meetings in which the staff actively anticipated the introduction
of the National Curriculum. These meetings were characterized by
swings between bitterness, anger and optimism, between hostility,
anxiety and purposeful hope. Out of them, and other related activities,
came a sense, in the words of one teacher, that 'we're making the
National Curriculum part of what *we* want to do'. During 1989–90, I
listened to a headteacher in inner London talking about an idiosyncratic
INSET day which he and all the staff, teaching and non-teaching, had
organized and participated in before the start of the autumn term. He
finished by saying, 'at the end of it I saw that what we had been doing
was mourning the death of ILEA and yet reaffirming the fact that, as
a school, we would still go on'. Whether or not they realize it, I think
that in the past few years many school staffs have been providing
themselves with the opportunity to work constructively through their
grief in formalized stages and that these have given a meaningful
structure to a transition whose outcomes are still unknown. Whether
other educationalists, such as administrators and inspectors, have been
able to mourn together in the same way is much less clear.

My second point is related to this. Although bereavement may be
experienced collectively, its impact is always individual. We have to

make sense of loss in the light of our own experience. We may share in the expression of others' grief, but we cannot participate in their making of renewed meaning, since this must by definition be personal. It follows that we can best help the successful resolution of grieving by allowing individuals to take charge of their own recovery. This is not always easy. The instinct to offer help, especially marked among client-centred professionals, may be compounded by a desire to reconstitute our own meaning and purposes through the exercise of control over others. Yet they themselves cannot establish fresh identities unless they are given freedom and encouragement to work through their own inner conflicts and to find their own ways of piecing their idiosyncratic experience together again in a form that makes sense to them. In practical terms, this means that we have to tread a difficult balance between on the one hand offering companionship, support, a sense of continuity with the past and on the other allowing the bereaved to make their own decisions, to take renewed control of their own lives. This balance reflects the ambivalence of grief itself. It may be the more difficult to achieve if we ourselves are grieving for the loss of our own sense of self. The task of helping ourselves through the ambivalence of grief while also offering constructive assistance to our colleagues is one which calls for sensitivity, restraint and patience, at the very time when we are likely to be especially short of these qualities. I think there is room in the education system at present for the services of impartial strangers, skilled in counselling or, at least, in listening. In the period 1988–90 one authority at least was prepared to pay for its headteachers to talk to such a counsellor, for a limited number of hours. Three others appointed career counsellors available to all school staff on request.

Such adaptive responses were encouraging. They represented an insightful and constructive use of collective resources which seemed likely to assist the service as a whole towards a renewed sense of energy and purpose. However, more recently the erosion of authority budgets has made it more difficult for them to fund corporate services of this kind, and the teachers' access to them has declined as a result.

Third, the negotiation of an altered identity requires time as well as sympathetic, non-obtrusive support. It cannot be hurried. Indeed, the message of Marris and others is clear: grieving is a process which must work itself out. If it is aborted, either by an unchallenged clinging to the past, or by an unthinking leap into the future, the embryonic new self is unlikely to survive.

Yet time, it seems at present, is the commodity of which the education service is most short. Nor, as we are hurried along by the consequences of changing legislation, does there seem much prospect of finding it. The costs are clear, in terms of emotional pressure, health, requests for early retirement, teacher shortages, mounting apathy and cynicism. I do not know how we persuade policy-makers that members of the educational system, and here I would include parents and governors, need time to assimilate the changes of the past few years and constructively to recreate from them their own sense of professional meaning. My belief, based in part on my current work with teachers, advisers, inspectors and administrators, is that some of those who have to implement these changes will, in the absence of 'government time', make it for themselves, by fending off the impact of intended innovations in a multitude of bureaucratic, unofficial or personal ways.

Lastly, to view radical educational change as bereavement and accommodation to it as the gradual construction of a new self-conception is to stress the part played in this process by significant others and reference groups. Although the meaning of loss and the way in which past, present and future are reintegrated are unique to each individual, this does not mean that recovery is a solitary process. On the contrary, our substantial selves are formed by the expectations others have of us and the reinforcement that they give us. So, when an important part of the self is lost, we need interaction with others to help in the process of reconstruction. In Nias (1987a), summarized in Nias (1987b), I drew upon the work of S.H. Foulkes, a group psychotherapist whose intellectual and social roots were in the Frankfurt School of critical theory and of M.J. Abercrombie, a zoologist and a medical and architectural educator, to interpret the way in which over long periods of time freely formed groups of teachers spontaneously used discussion to change their own and one another's perspectives and opinions. The members of such groups not only supported one another but, more importantly, also challenged one another's basic assumptions, self-perceptions and behaviour towards others. As they talked to one another and interacted non-verbally, building mutual support and overcoming conflict, pain and resistance, they began, severally and together, to force upon one another 'decisive changes in experience and behaviour' (Foulkes, 1975, p. 62). Foulkes saw this process of group interaction, which he called 'ego-training in action' as being 'the most powerful factor in bringing about change and the possibility for further and future progress after the group has ended' (Foulkes, 1975, p. 63). The teachers whose professional lives are reported in Nias (1989) also saw their experience in the groups to which they had belonged as being of paramount importance in helping them to modify, or even drastically to change, their view of themselves as practitioners. As one said of her group membership, it was 'probably the most important and formative experience I've ever had'.

Although both Foulkes and Abercrombie deliberately set up such discussion groups (for psychotherapeutic and educational purposes, respectively), the teachers who reported their experience to me had come together accidentally, drawn together by proximity and commitment to a common task. The groups varied in size between three and eight, being big enough to provide a diversity of views but small enough for everyone to be heard. Otherwise, they were all characterized by equal power relations, by discussion of members' own concerns, by a willingness to expose, through talking, their differences in prespective and practice and by mutual support for one another's attempts to bring about changes in the way each saw him/herself as a teacher.

Lack of time and opportunity to meet make it hard for such groups to flourish in schools. Yet with some encouragement, such as that provided by INSET days or curriculum working parties, they could be commoner than they are. The kind of developments most obviously needed are: acceptance by headteachers and administrators that discussion of teachers' own concerns is a worthwhile professional activity, and provision of more time within the school day for talking; encouragement of contexts (such as open-plan units, team teaching, shared curriculum responsibilities) in which shared coping brings small groups of people together with common starting points for discussion; recruitment for diversity and organizational provision (perhaps through interdepartmental working parties) for its expression; acceptance at all levels of the educational system of the value of disagreement, set within a secure environment; provision in all kinds of teacher education for open discussion and the sharing of perspectives; emphasis within management training upon the need to reduce hierarchical practices and encourage collegial discussion, and to develop leaders who will listen and support without losing their power to help individuals uncover their own basic assumptions or, when necessary, to protect them from the group; acceptance by teachers of the need for open supportive discussion among peers and a willingness to give their time to it.

To sum up, I have drawn upon a longitudinal study of primary teachers to show that the work in which they are engaged calls for a high level of self-investment, with the result that for many of them personal and professional identity become fused; the teacher is the person, and an important part of the person is the teacher. I have then used Marris' work on personal and social change to show that recent innovations have had an effect upon many educationalists which can be interpreted as bereavement, that is as such a radical loss of the structures which give their lives meaning that change seems like a loss of self. Bereavement can be resolved by a redefinition of meaning in a way which integrates past, present and future, but this process involves grieving which is itself contradictory and painful. Lastly, I have suggested ways in which educationalists might help themselves and others to find a constructive resolution to professional grief: by accepting its threatening and conflictual nature, and by making provision for the expression of feeling; by allowing individuals to take charge of their own recovery; by encouraging people to provide one another with support and challenge as together they negotiate the slow, difficult path of constructing fresh identities. What I have not been able to suggest is where or how, in the present political and economic climate, we find the time which is needed for grief to be constructively worked out, and for fresh self-conceptions to be pieced together. Yet on this the success or failure of recent innovations may ultimately depend. Unless teachers and other educationalists are given time to assimilate change and the stresses it brings, to accommodate purposefully to a new professional world and to re-establish a sense of control over it, bereavement may be followed not by the creation of new identities but by debilitating passivity, angry fear or in the end by the silence of complete disintegration.

## References

ABERCROMBIE, M.L.J. (1969) *The Anatomy of Judgement: An Investigation into the Processes of Perception and Reasoning*, Harmondsworth, Penguin.

ALEXANDER, R. (1984) *Primary Teaching*, London, Cassell.

ARGYRIS, C. (1964) *Integrating the Individual and the Organization*, New York, Wiley.

BETTELHEIM, B. (1961) *The Informed Heart*, London, Thames & Hudson.

CONNELL, R. (1985) *Teachers' Work*, London, Allen & Unwin.

DELAMONT, S. (1987) 'The primary teacher, 1945–1990: Myths and realities', in DELAMONT, S. (Ed.) *The Primary School Teacher*, London, Falmer Press.

DEPARTMENT OF EDUCATION AND SCIENCE (1982) *The New Teacher in School*, HMI Series: Matters for Discussion, 15, London, HMSO.

DEPARTMENT OF EDUCATION AND SCIENCE (1983) *Teaching Quality*, London, HMSO.

FOULKES, S.H. (1975) 'A short outline of the therapeutic processes in group-analytic psychotherapy', *Group Analysis*, **8**, pp. 59–63.

GOFFMAN, E. (1968) *Asylums*, Harmondsworth, Penguin.

HARGREAVES, D. (1980) 'The occupational culture of teachers', in WOODS, P. (Ed.) *Teacher Strategies: Explorations in the Sociology of the School*, London, Croom Helm.

LORTIE, D. (1975) *School Teacher: A Sociological Study*, Chicago, University of Chicago Press.

MARRIS, P. (1958) *Widows and Their Families*, London, Routledge.

MARRIS, P. (1986) *Loss and Change*, 2nd edn, London, Routledge.

NIAS, J. (1987a) *Seeing Anew: Teachers' Theories of Teaching and Learning*, Geelong, Deakin University Press.

NIAS, J. (1987b) 'Learning from difference', in SMYTH, W.J. (Ed.) *Educating Teachers: Changing the Nature of Pedagogical Knowledge*, London, Falmer Press.

NIAS, J. (1989) *Primary Teachers Talking: A Study of Teaching as Work*, London, Routledge.

NIAS, J. (1992) 'Primary teachers talking: A reflexive account of longitudinal research', in WALFORD, G. (Ed.) *Doing Educational Research*, London, Routledge.

NIAS, J., SOUTHWORTH, G. and CAMPBELL, P. (1992) *Whole School Curriculum Development In The Primary School*, London, Falmer Press.

NIAS, J., SOUTHWORTH, G. and YEOMANS, R. (1989) *Staff Relationships in Primary Schools: A Study of Organizational Cultures*, London, Cassell.

POLLARD, A. (1985) *The Social World of the Primary School*, London, Cassell.

SIKES, P., MEASOR, L. and WOODS, P. (1985) *Teachers' Careers: Crises and Continuities*, London, Falmer Press.

WOODS, P. (1981) 'Strategies, commitment and identity: Making and breaking the teacher role', in BARTON, L. and WALKER, S. (Eds) *School Teachers and Teaching*, London, Falmer Press.

# 10 Educational Research and Professional Development: On Minds that Watch Themselves

*Mary Louise Holly*

## Introduction

So the journey is over and I am back again, richer by much experience and poorer by many exploded convictions, many perished certainties. For convictions and certainties are too often the concomitants of ignorance . . . I set out on my travels knowing, or thinking I knew, how men should live, how be governed, how educated, what they should believe. . . . Now . . . I find myself without any of these pleasing certainties. . . . The better you understand the significance of any question, the more difficult it becomes to answer it. Those who attach a high importance to their own opinion should stay at home. When one is travelling, convictions are mislaid as easily as spectacles, but unlike spectacles, they are not as easily replaced. (Aldous Huxley)

This chapter is about teachers' travelling, about where they go when they consciously keep track of themselves and inquire into their teaching. It explores relationships between educational inquiry and professional development. Development implies growth and change; research implies systematic self-critical inquiry. Professional researchers and professional teachers can be described as: thoughtful, inquisitive, disciplined, open-minded, sceptical, hospitable to unexpected and disconfirming data, informed and knowledgeable, imaginative and flexible, with observation skills and confidence. To teach, it is argued here, is to inquire. As teachers conduct research, they formatively evaluate their work, theorize and test their ideas in practice. As they learn more about the subject of their inquiry, they also discover more about themselves and processes of inquiry. The questions teachers pose and the methods they use depend on their cognitive functioning, psychological health and maturity, and the contexts of their practice.

School reform takes place on multiple levels and dimensions and teachers are a vital and necessary part of the processes of evaluation and reform. Practitioner knowledge 'is a central part of the evaluation process' and 'teachers can enable other teachers to take a critical look at this knowledge base' (Gitlin, 1989, p. 322). Observing and describing practitioner knowledge is not an easy task though. As Hartley and Broadfoot (1988) have cautioned, there are many difficulties in developing methods of assessing teachers, not the least of which are observation schemes (Day, 1987). Policies which shape evaluation must reflect consideration of the social nature of change, the nature of teaching (Darling-Hammond, Wise and Pease, 1986), and the nature of personal and professional development (Elliott, 1989a). If teachers are to understand the world of the school and to contribute to educational change, the systematic self-critical inquiry necessary to professional practice (Stenhouse, 1975) must be supported by school environments which are hospitable to their research. Conditions of practice and policies which continue to contribute to the maintenance of teachers at a survival level (low in risk taking, conservative, present oriented and self-judgmental rather than self-accepting; Lortie, 1975), make change highly unlikely if not impossible. Teachers' images of themselves, their attitudes toward research, and the conditions of practice will have to change in order for teachers to *be* researchers. Understanding *how* teachers theorize, or, as Weston (1979) phrased it, how teachers determine 'what is happening' is an initial step in developing appropriate support systems for formative evaluation, research, and professional development.

The purpose of this chapter is to discuss examples of teachers' educational inquiry, of how they formatively evaluate and change their practice, and to place these within a context of personal, professional development. My purpose in conducting the research on which this chapter is based was to gain insights and understanding into the processes of teachers' professional development, in particular to describe their thinking as they come to terms with the challenges of teaching and themselves as professionals. How do teachers grow and change as they teach? What are the dilemmas they choose to investigate and how do they investigate them? How do teachers learn about their practice, themselves, the contexts of schooling? In what ways do they question these contexts, themselves and their practice? How do they come to realizations which they might prefer not to encounter? In what ways do they come to know, accept, and change their practice, and their conceptions of teaching and schooling?

After a brief description of the studies from which the teachers' inquiry presented here are drawn, there is a section on 'Educational Research and an Attitude of Scientific Inquiry'. The chapter then addresses 'Professional Development' from several theoretical perspectives. 'Teachers' Inquiry' is discussed using excerpts from teachers' journals. The chapter concludes with a summary and the premise of the chapter, namely, that inquiry (and theorizing) is inherent in teaching, that teachers must take themselves into account in studying practice, and that the degree to which teachers are able to conduct such inquiry depends upon and influences their professional development and the contexts within which they practice.

## Reflections on Practice: Studies of Teacher Theorizing

'Teacher Reflections on Classroom Life: An Empirical Base for Professional Development' was the title of a year-long research project funded by the National Institute of Education to study teaching from the teacher's perspective. For over a year seven primary school teachers kept open-ended journals, met weekly for two and one-half hours during the academic year for a seminar on teaching and professional development which evolved from their interests, and included me as a participant observer in their classrooms for three to four hours every other week.

Teachers had to become researchers into their own practice. The process of reflecting, especially in writing, was difficult. Data analysis was difficult too; as one kindergarten teacher put it, 'how often my perceptions were tied to other things than the immediate circumstances. Black can be white.' Inquiry was everywhere in teaching. It was a constant process of posing questions and responding to them; of making split second decisions with a myriad of 'twenty-second holocausts' throughout the teaching day. Incongruities, and contradictions became harder to ignore: 'When I write something, it becomes a contract with myself'.

Similar discomforts with reflective inquiry were experienced by teachers in a year-long study of beginning teachers (see Holly, 1989). As the project progressed, more guided journal writing was introduced. The third study from which this chapter draws is of teachers' research journals written as part of two graduate courses ('Field Based Professional Development'; 'Teachers' Theories of Action') offered at Deakin University in Victoria, Australia. These journals were focused mainly on a research project of the teachers' choice.

### Educational Research and an Attitude of Scientific Inquiry

> What we observe is not nature itself, but nature exposed to our methods of questioning. . . . Natural science does not simply describe and explain nature, it is part of the interplay between nature and ourselves. (Werner Heisenberg)

Research is 'study and investigation, esp. to discover new facts', 'to search into (a matter or subject) to investigate or study closely', 'aimed at discovery and interpretation of new facts', and 'to search again' (*Oxford English Dictionary*). 'Research' and 'practice' are often seen as separate processes (which they often are) conducted by different people — researchers and teachers. Until recently, teacher researchers were little more than a chapter heading in Lawrence Stenhouse's book, *An Introduction to Curriculum Research and Development* (1975). Now, there is an increasing cadre of educational researchers who suggest that teaching itself should be construed as a form of educational research rather than its object. That, 'educational inquiry is not a separate process from the practice of education. It is a form of reflective practice' (Elliott, 1989b, p. 83).

Reflective practice implies conscious and thoughtful action, which, according to Dewey (1961), is the opposite of 'routine and capricious behaviour' which refuses 'to acknowledge responsibility for the future consequences which flow from present action. Reflection is the acceptance of such responsibility' (p. 146). Teachers have little choice in accepting the responsibility of reflective practice:

> When the subject matter with which the scientist [teacher] deals consists of human beings trying to act effectively to carry out their purposes, then the social responsibility of anyone who pretends to be an expert obviously becomes very great indeed (Cantril *et al.*, 1949, p. 19).

For this reason teaching has been described as a moral science (Elliott, 1989a) and as a moral craft (Tom, 1980); it presupposes something of value will be taught (Peters, 1965) and it is inherently unequal in the relationship of teacher to student (Tom, 1980). 'How do I improve my practice?' (Whitehead, 1989) carries with it the implicit responsibility to study oneself in the process. Teachers (and scientific researchers) create their worlds as they interpret them. Cantril (*et al.*, 1949) notes the importance of the lenses which interpreters bring to their investigations.

> What man [*sic*] brings to any concrete event is an accumulation of assumptions, of awarenesses, and of knowledge . . . derived from his past experiences. But since the environment . . . is constantly changing, any person is constantly running into hitches and trying to do away with them. The assumptive world a person brings to the 'now' of a concrete situation cannot disclose to him the undetermined significances continually emerging and so we run into hitches in everyday life . . . and our ability to act effectively for a purpose becomes inadequate.
>
> When we try to grasp this inadequacy intellectually and get at the 'why' of the ineffectiveness of our purposeful action, we are adopting an attitude of scientific inquiry (p. 12).

To neglect the background of the researcher is to jeopardize and to 'sterilize not only the process but also the results of inquiry' (Herrick, 1949, p. 180f).

## Professional Development

The term 'development' can be defined as 'a gradual unfolding, a bringing into fuller view; bringing out latent capabilities of; a fuller expansion. Gradual advancement through progressive stages, growth from within' (*Oxford English Dictionary*). The question in teaching becomes, 'Development toward what?'

### Teacher Professional Development

Addressing herself to the adult development of teachers, Oja (1989) outlines three areas for growth:

> *Ego Maturity* — The development of more complex, differentiated, and integrated understanding of self and others, away from

manipulative, exploitative, self-protective attitudes toward self-respect, mutual respect, and identity formation.

*Moral/Ethical Development* — Development toward principled moral judgments, away from unquestioned conformity to peer, social, and legal norms *toward* self-evaluated standards within a world view framework cherishing individual human rights and mutual interpersonal responsibilities.

*Conceptual Growth* — The development of higher conceptual levels, away from thinking in terms of simple stereotypes and cliches *toward* recognition of individual differences in attitudes, interests, and abilities, and toward increased toleration for paradox, contradiction and ambiguity (p. 151).

From a plethora of theories of human development, a few which relate to teachers' evolving capacities as inquirers are discussed here: perceptual, cognitive, psychoanalytic and humanistic theories.

### Construct Theory and Perceptual Approaches to Development

According to construct theory (Kelly, 1955), we have and construct mental schemata (conceptual maps) which help us to adapt, interpret, and understand the world and our experiences. People have permeable or impermeable cognitive constructs depending on their views of themselves in particular circumstances: if a person feels threatened, the constructs narrow, if a person feels at ease, the constructs are more permeable. The expression that 'when you are up to your ass in alligators you won't think of draining the swamp' illustrates this concept. Gliding through the water in a big, safe boat, your constructs (and vision) can be open to varieties of water life which you missed while you were trying to survive in the thick of it.

Combs and Snygg (1959) put forth a related theory. From a perceptual perspective the one basic need which underlies motivation is maintaining and developing an adequate self (pp. 44–45). Learning and knowledge are useful only to the extent that they are perceived to contribute to maintaining and developing personal adequacy. As did Kelly, Combs and Snygg find that 'People under threat are likely to behave rigidly and unquestioningly' (p. 189). From this view of development, 'all behavior, without exception, is completely determined by, and pertinent to, the perceptual field of the behaving organism' (p. 20)

The perceptual field is the entire universe, including the self, 'as it is experienced by the individual at the instant of action' (Combs and Snygg, 1959). It has three main characteristics: it is *fluid and continually changing*, it has *stability*, and it has *direction*. Even if a person's behaviour resists any logical or obvious rationale to us (or to the person), our perceptions 'are never masses of meaningless and unrelated stimuli' (Combs and Snygg, 1959, pp. 23–24). Behaviour then, is a function of a person's perceptions of an external event rather than a function of the event itself (p. 21). 'It is what the person *sees* that is enabling or disabling. The crucial matter is not so much what you are, but what you think you are' (Kelley, 1962, pp. 9–10).

At the centre of the perceptual field lies the phenomenal self which is constructed in relationship with others. It 'consists of an organization of accumulated experience over a whole lifetime' and, because it develops in social relationships, it must be achieved (Kelley, 1962). As Kelley notes: 'A great deal of the self has been relegated to the unconscious' and continues to function 'for weal or woe, depending on the quality of experiences' (1962).

The way one sees oneself then, determines action. From his study of human motivations, Maslow (1968) conceptualized a hierarchy of seven needs. The first four — physiological, safety, love and belonging, and esteem — are *deficiency* needs (D needs) because they produce an unpleasant tension which can only be reduced or met by an outside person. Self-actualization, desire to know and understand, and aesthetic needs are *being* needs (B needs) because they are associated with pleasurable tensions and can be met by the person herself or himself. With B needs the person is free to perceive more of 'what is' rather than what one *needs* to see. D needs must be satisfied to ensure survival whereas B needs contribute to enjoyment, understanding, and creativity in life. What we learn depends upon what we need to learn.

Construct theory and perceptual approaches to development are consistent with notions explored by researchers in teacher development. Fuller (1969), for example, describes three stages of teacher development: first the survival stage where the teacher's main concern is with survival and preservation of self; second, the main concern is with mastering teaching, and in the third, with the impact and influence on students' learning and development of both the curriculum and teaching. Here we find an example of teachers working to *maintain* an adequate self in the first stage and in the second and third, to *develop* and extend their professional selves. In Maslow's terms, once they have survived and feel as if they belong in the profession, they are free to develop. As one need in the hierarchy is satisfied, another need can come into focus (Maslow, 1968). These needs reappear when persons find themselves in new and different life situations (such as a new job, a new family group). Fuller's stages are not inevitable; a different form of teacher preparation might yield different results; beginning teachers need not join a profession where they fear for their survival.

In times of obvious transition we try to maintain stability yet we also cannot enjoy the comfort of schemata which no longer make sense to us. The dilemma makes itself felt in our behaviour and in our inner conversations with ourselves.

### *Becoming Conscious: On Cognition and Multiminds*

Who is minding the store? The discomfort of development is in part due to outer and inner battles for centre stage, for focusing attention. Our sensory systems exist to act as filters to discard irrelevant information 'to protect us from being overwhelmed and confused by this mass of information' (Ornstein, 1986, p. 24). Seeing entails the visual experience of the eye telling the brain what's out there, and of the brain telling the eye what it sees. As information travels to the visual cortex, it is increasingly simplified and abstracted. What becomes part of the perceptual field represents a fraction of what might be included (Ornstein, 1986).

Humankind differs from other organisms in that our avenues to sensation are more complex, multimodal, and flexible. The frog, for example, has developed vision to take into account only four different messages, one of them being to respond to bugs flying around it, obviously an asset to its survival. No matter how complex the environment of the frog, it is wired to react only to those four stimuli. The frog doesn't stop and think, 'Oh! There is a bug and I am hungry!' nor does it prefer to wait for a more tasty dinner. It simply sees and reacts automatically. We, on the other hand, can 'tune ourselves continuously to suit our needs and expectations . . . but we are not usually *aware* of such self-tuning' (Ornstein, 1986, p. 29). We may forego one dinner opportunity for another.

We act on partial pictures (our theories) and fill in the missing parts. Filling in means seeking that which makes the subject or picture harmonious. 'The harmony is found to consist in having outer experiences meet our expectations' (Stratton, 1896). This harmony necessitates orchestrating and integrating multiple selves, or minds. Ornstein (1987) explains that

the mind is diverse and complex . . . a changeable conglomer-
ation of different kinds of 'small minds' — fixed reactions,
talents, flexible thinking and these . . . are temporarily employed
— 'wheeled into consciousness' — then usually discarded,
returned to their place, after use (p. 25).

Which small mind is wheeled in depends upon the perceptual field and
perceived need. Yet, unlike frogs, we can become conscious of our
small minds and intervene in the selection of which will prevail. One
might say that there are many small voices inside giving advice, each
lobbying for its own point of view and values. Take the hungry frog:
it has no choice, there is one voice. Now consider Martha, a hungry
human being. The conversation of her minds might be something like
this:

(mind 1)   I want some food *now*!
(m2)   How about stopping for a hot fudge sundae?
(m1)   Peanut butter crackers from the machine are faster!
(m2)   But not nearly as delicious!
(m3)   Hey you guys! How about waiting ten minutes till we
        get home and you can have some of that nutritious
        spinach salad?
(m2)   Delicious? Compared to a hot fudge sundae? Who are
        you trying to kid?
(m3)   You'll only be uncomfortably full and regret it.
(m5)   Don't blame me when you can't button your pants.
(m4)   And think about your teeth!
(m1)   Ok you guys. Knock it off. While you debate, I'm
        starving to death. How about stopping on the way home
        for a low fat frozen yogurt?
(m2,3,5,4)   Not a bad idea, considering . . .
(m4)   Just make sure it's sweetened with fruit.

According to Ornstein, the observer mind, the ability to observe
this inner conversation going on, is a dormant faculty in most of us
simply because we have no cause to notice the different minds taking
control at any time. Yet, it can be developed 'by first observing the
alternations, gradations, and changes that "come over" us; then noting
that it is not always necessary to accept the multimind that is "automatically" called up in a situation' (Ornstein, 1987, p. 185). It becomes
a matter of 'who is running the show?'

We are built to respond simply and quickly . . . primed to respond to what's on at the moment and sometimes we over-react. We are primed by emotions to alertness or action to avoid emergencies . . . constant problems get ignored . . . we remain unaware because we do not understand the complexity within ourselves . . . the separated components of the mind (p. 32).

### Becoming Integrated: Psychosynthesis and Many Selves

Looking at the various roles we play (child, parent, friend, teacher, adviser, colleague, advocate), it is not difficult to see how some sub-personalities (Assagioli, 1973) might develop, and others might not. With the same ultimate aim that Ornstein articulates in cognitive psychology, psychosynthesis (a form of psychoanalytic theory) points the person toward self-understanding through observation — activating the 'observer mind' so that unconscious selves can be brought into consciousness. The frog has no such difficulties! A goal of psychosynthesis is to observe oneself without being emotionally attached to what one sees. This process is called dis-identification: 'Because we all have a tendency to identify with . . . this or that subpersonality, we come to believe that we *are* it. Dis-identification consists of our snapping out of this illusion . . . It is often accompanied by a sense of insight and liberation' (Ferrucci, 1982, p. 49).

The problem with emotional attachment and identification is that one attaches one's self-esteem to this and is affected by its state. For example, as a teacher it is important for me to be able to understand a child's point of view, and if I can feel like the child, to the degree that this is possible, I am in a better position to provide support and encouragement that will fit the circumstances. However, when I cannot step outside of the child's point of view, I am a captive of it; I cannot observe from multiple perspectives; if the child is sad, I am sad. A teacher can, on a hectic day, move from one identification to another, one crisis to another without ever stepping out of the action long enough to catch her or his bearings (dis-identify).

### Individuation

Susanne Langer, in *Mind: An Essay on Human Feeling* (1982) describes how civilizations develop some attributes and not others, how, for example, Australian aboriginals have highly developed the spiritual nature of their culture whereas the United States has highly developed the technological nature of its society. In contrast, technology has not been developed to a high level in the aboriginal society and spiritual life has not been developed to a high degree in the USA.

Embedded in Jung's concept of individuation is a similar point: we develop those aspects of ourselves which appear to be most adaptive to our survival and growth and we neglect other aspects. Individuation means integrating and developing these various aspects of ourselves: 'It is not merely the "shadow" side of our personalities that we overlook, disregard, and repress. We may also do the same thing to our positive qualities' (Jung, 1968, p. 51). The process of individuation is made possible when the individual stops trying to control what is unconscious and steps out of the way simply to observe those aspects of the self that seek to be recognized (von Franz, 1968, p. 165). Projection onto others is often a step in individuation. In teachers' journal writing, for example, the writer will often note a problem with a colleague, and only later realize that 'I have this problem!' As Ferrucci (1982, p. 42) notes, recognizing (observing) the problem is the first step, 'for any pattern that is discovered — and fully faced changes'.

### Psychological Health and Creativity

Addressing teacher professional development, Heath (1980) and others (Hunt, 1970, Oja and Pine, 1983; Oja, 1989; Sprinthall and Sprinthall, 1982) argue that levels of conceptual development and psychological maturity are better predictors of adult functioning than are the usual measures of adult academic achievement and intelligence. Heath defines several characteristics of psychological maturity in educators: the ability to symbolize experience, reflectivity, self-awareness, ability to take multiple and other views, to understand others empathetically, to think analytically and logically, predict, more tolerance and understanding of others, better personal integration, more consistent values, and the ability to establish reciprocally mutual and cooperative relationships. Psychologically mature people are more stable, less disrupted by personal stress and bias, and are more autonomous and self-reliant than less psychologically mature individuals (Heath, 1980, p. 201). To foster these characteristics Heath advocates an 'educational environment that involves the values, interpersonal skills, and self-concepts of teachers as well as their knowledge and cognitive skills' (p. 204).

Psychological health is related to creativity (Maslow, 1968; May, 1975; Jung, 1968; Hillman, 1983; Arieti, 1976). According to Maslow (1954), 'every person is, in part, "his own project" [*sic*] and makes himself'. Creativity is a normal manifestation of psychological health. It is not something that one possesses or does not possess, nor is it a measurable trait. There are many shared characteristics with psychological maturity as defined by Heath above: a youthful attitude, self-confidence and autonomy, openness to experience, tolerance for ambiguity, humour, and childlikeness (Lugo and Hershey, 1979).

Ashley Montagu (1989) argues that in 'body, spirit, feeling, and conduct we are designed to grow and develop in ways that emphasize rather than minimize childlike traits' (p. 2). Montagu argues for many characteristics which are necessary for a researcher: 'curiosity is one of the most important; imaginativeness; playfulness; open-mindedness; willingness to experiment; flexibility; humor; energy; receptiveness to new ideas; honesty; eagerness to learn . . .' (p. 2). Divergent thinking, characteristic of children and of adults who are described as creative, is necessary for adaptation and change, and teaching demands this in abundance. The question is how to promote the development of these qualities?

### Teachers' Inquiry

> . . . intelligence in action is ultimately a function of the whole of what we are. Truth in the big picture is an inherently participatory measure: it is a measure not just of things, but of relationships between things, and one of the key relationships is that between ourselves and what we are measuring (Johnston, 1986, p. 41).

#### Beginning Teachers' Inquiry

When teachers document their practice they find that their interpretations change with time and psychological distance, that their realities (perceptual fields) change with their personal 'life projects' or 'developmental tasks'. One beginning teacher, for example, observed her journal writing and discussion of teaching in a seminar group and found 'I'm stuck on survival', while other teachers had moved beyond this 'survival stage' (Fuller, 1969). Listening to other beginning teachers discuss teaching alerted her to considerations beyond herself. As this group of teachers discussed their teaching they found that they viewed children's behaviour in different ways: for Barb, Paul's inattentiveness meant 'I am failing'; for Sally, it meant 'He has reasons . . .'; while for Connie it meant 'We're not connecting'. How they approached this hitch in practice depended on their individual perceptual worlds and their view of themselves in relation to Paul and teaching.

Beginning teachers at the reception level had difficulties related to transitions. Both the children and the teachers were going through major transitions. 'How do I know I am a good teacher?' alternates with questions and discomforts in helping the children through transitions.

> My kids were really wound up today; I had to really exercise my patience . . .
>
> I think part of the reason they are so restless is that they are experiencing a change in routine . . . I am trying to revise my seatwork routine *away* from dittos and *toward* other things. So right now I'm sort of floating in between, and they are probably wondering a bit about why things are different.

Early childhood teachers' journals also contained more mention and concern for parent–teacher conferences than did those of more experienced and upper grade level teachers. Age was frequently alluded to, with young teachers feeling too young and inexperienced to act as experts on children and their learning — especially to parents. Evaluation was a particularly troublesome and oft written about responsibility. Observation related to action research proved to be useful. In this excerpt a teacher tries to record a child's behaviour so she can approach her difficulties with his motivation and behaviour systematically. She begins with a description of the problems, then documents his behaviour over several days (only part of one day is excerpted here), and concludes with an interpretation.

2/6
Jason is one of the two white children in our class . . . is slightly overweight and is of average height . . . a little more intellectual than most in our class. He enjoys things that lead to enquiry and creativity. Jason does not like to do things that are not to his liking . . . verbal complaints are common when this occurs . . . I have tried seating him in various ways and in a matter of time he is begging to be moved. Verbal arguments

are very frequent. Outbursts about how he hates our class [are] common. Twice he has cried over his lack of friends . . .

2/11
| | | |
|---|---|---|
| 10:30 | Created a detailed pattern for his haiku. | |
| 12:00 | On task–No arguing. | |
| 1:30 | Came back from lunch upset–wouldn't say why. | |
| 2:30 | Helping him clean out his desk, I saw a note that was complaining about school and me. | |
| | Got immediately upset when he realized I saw it . . . | |

I assume something must have happened on the playground. Although, reflecting back, he seemed to get himself under control again.

The factor that seemed to initiate his poor behavior was when I saw the note he had written.

As Trudy logs Jason's behaviour she begins to observe in a more detached, less emotional way than when she simply reacts. She observes in greater detail and finds patterns and connections in events as she responds to the queries from her observations. She notes, for example, when Jason is 'on task' — which is surprisingly often. She documents her actions. Trudy analyzes her observations and questions with a colleague who poses questions of her: 'What do you mean by he is "more intellectual than most"?'

Time management, organization and tensions in teaching were recurrent observations.

I found many differences in my writing throughout the year . . . in . . . my attitude. I find that immediately following a weekend (time to 'catch up' and organization) I am very optimistic, however throughout the week I become a little more pessimistic with each day. I also found that I continually speak of time management and organization. . . . My writings seem very defensive at the beginning of the year compared to now. I guess a little experience can really change your views. I also noticed that in the first few months my writings were very stressful and now I'm more at ease. When I was reading these I almost seemed like another person, and the things that seemed *so* important then aren't *so* important now. I'll bet if I kept track of everyday personal life I would see the same pattern.

For many beginning teachers the adaptation to teaching has reverberations throughout the year.

> Monday, Feb 2
>
> I'm still feeling as though I need to make a number of changes in what I'm doing right now. For one thing, I need to get a better handle on my discipline procedures instead of the more 'on-the-spot' tactics I have now . . . teacher fantasy is getting abolished by reality!
>
> Also, my questioning techniques need to be refined, and I need to mix in some higher level questions with what I am doing now.
>
> *Also also* — I need to get more away from ditto work — I'm trying this now.
>
> And — my room needs to be more organized and clean and bulletin boards and learning centers changed more often.

One week before the above was written, Julie, the teacher, had her second principal's evaluation of her teaching, which was quite favourable; still she began to see things that could be improved. Many areas of concern that Julie and other beginning teachers allude to are also found in experienced teachers' journals.

*Inquiry to Improve Practice: Experienced Teachers' Theorizing*

Most teachers inquire into technical aspects of teaching when they begin to consciously and systematically explore practice. Just as Julie and other beginning teachers try to improve their question-asking techniques, so do experienced teachers. The following excerpts are from Sister Mary Beth's journal which she kept in conjunction with a graduate course at an Australian university. She has selected aspects of teaching to study and two of these areas and excerpts from her journal discussion about them are presented here.

> One of the aspects of my teaching I wanted to improve was questioning. From a technical point of view I wanted to improve this mode of behaviour . . .
>
> *Hidden Agenda*
> . . . I am trying to examine the motives and look at the history behind my rationale . . .

. . . I thought I would like to improve my skills in questioning . . . I found that I wanted to improve this technique so that I would have greater control over the group of children.

I am a very authoritarian teacher and I don't like interruptions or very much movement while I am teaching . . . I find it hard to cope with group work and I like to teach the class as a whole. I had open admiration for my colleague who attempted group work very successfully . . . after twenty years of teaching 'ingrained' habits and attitudes die hard. When I first began teaching the sign of a good teacher was a quiet class-room regardless of whether the children were learning anything or just sitting passively there like lumps. It is also difficult to change . . . even though you know that there could be better ways . . .

I first began to look for the hidden agenda when my colleague told me that I had asked the questions well. I remember thinking, well where do I go from here? . . . I realized that many teachers perfect the art of asking skilled questions but how many ask why do we perfect this technique? I would imagine that more hidden agendas will come to light . . .

### Explaining
The second aspect of my teaching which I chose . . . was the skill of explanation . . .

### Hidden Agenda
. . . one of the reasons again is to have complete control. . . . Even though part of my mind knows that children do not sit passively all day in order to learn something, I find that I still insist on complete order and control. I realized this when I reflected on one of the lessons I gave on a wet and windy day. I thought there would be chaos in the room, so I was much more directive throughout the lesson and felt ill at ease when the principal came in to count heads to see who was going to the visiting theatre group . . . . The librarian then appeared, so amid the interruptions the lesson proceeded.

The children were not at all disturbed by the visitors but I could feel my own uncomfortableness and a sense of a loss of control. This loss of control was not evident to anyone but myself.

Sister Mary Beth continues her journal by looking at the history of evaluation and the terror which strikes when she hears, 'The inspector is coming soon'.

> This is the dreaded statement which every teacher shudders upon hearing. Suddenly programs are brought up to date, the school is cleaned beyond recognition and the students and their exercise books are suddenly neat and tidy. It certainly has never been a happy or helpful event for most schools. There is always the strong emphasis upon control and efficiency. Hence most teachers lock themselves in their class-rooms and generally shun all intruders. The obvious questions come to mind. How can teachers improve their skills? How will effective professional development of a lasting nature take place? . . . the traditional forms of supervision have created dependence, rather than independence.

Sister Mary Beth's reflections provide an example of a process which is documented in most teachers' research journals: what worked, or was taken for granted, no longer works or its use is questioned. A hitch interrupts the *status quo*. As Kuhn points out in *The Structure of Scientific Revolutions*, 'rules are derived from paradigms' (1962, p. 42). When the paradigm, or world view begins to change, the rules are no longer appropriate, yet the teacher doesn't have anything with which to replace them, the consequence not infrequently being that the teacher applies the old solution in spades: 'once engaged [in inquiry] what challenges him [*sic*] is the conviction that, if only he is skillful enough, he will succeed in solving a puzzle . . .' (Kuhn, 1962, p. 38). Teachers too approach their tasks 'hoping to find order' (Kuhn, 1962, p. 37).

When teachers undertake to inquire into their practice, what was safe and familiar becomes strange; a new paradigm is in the offing, but this is generally a real battle. 'Hanging on while letting go' was the way one teacher-administrator in Australia described his journey. After recounting several 'yesterdays' which were in every sense of the term 'Bloody Fridays!!!' where a group of children got the better of him and he 'blew my block and yelled at them', he reaches back into his own life experiences and reconstructs his childhood where he describes himself as a 'real bastard' — the same words he uses to describe the present young men he is trying to teach: 'They act like caged bastards!' He consistently and intently reconstructs his philosophy and laboriously tries out everything he can think of to tame the little bastards, making sure that his actions are congruent with his beliefs. The old world view just doesn't work: 'So what's happening?' As the fire on the pages of his journal relieve him of some of it, he is able to stand back, as Trudy did, and theorize: 'In 1966 I caned those type of students. In 1978 I kept them in and gave them lines. In 1986 I'm developing a strategy of "logical consequences" '.

David analyzes his teaching. He reads material related to teaching and finds an article which strikes a chord with his experience: teachers spend a significant amount of their time policing.

> The policemen, feeling that they must control and manipulate all situations involving students. Certainly, the comments in my journal indicated that this was my prime concern.

> '. . . act like caged bastards.'
> '. . . roam around the room, talk about everything else, annoy the class next door . . .'
> '. . . half of them wouldn't even listen to . . .'
> '. . . the kids virtually ignored me.'

> And I was concerned. I knew what I wanted them to do, and they wouldn't do it. What would the social ramifications be? What sort of principal would I be seen as?

Analyzing thirteen weeks of journal writing David decides that he is 'hanging on while letting go'. After he extinguishes all hope of prevailing with his philosophy and actions consistent with it, he gives up overt discipline (yelling at them) and concentrates on teaching the children who seem to be interested and ignores the rest, who, as it turns out, diminish in number.

### Writing, Contradictions, Expectations and Change

When teachers question and explore their practice, they run into contradictions and inconsistencies; they begin to state their expectations and the assumptions and beliefs which undergird their philosophies and actions. By putting their ideas and experiences on paper they give them more credibility and they capture them for later reflection and analysis. Focusing one's energies and attention on matters of consequence, no matter what these matters are, suggests to teachers that 'what I do matters'. Teacher researchers presented here ultimately confronted the questions of power, control, relevance, time and organization. The general pattern of gaining insight into themselves as teachers took place in the following sequence: curiosity, defining an area to study, finding contradictions and inconsistencies, trying new approaches after carefully re-trying old ones, coming to terms with their expectations, viewing students more as individuals and concomitantly reaching back into their own backgrounds and histories.

Judith Gates, an inspector in England, studied her own work for her master's thesis, and came to the realization that 'some principles are too precious to lose but too uncomfortable to keep . . . I have adopted several strategies to try to protect both my personal equilibrium and my professional self-esteem' (Gates, 1987). The multiple voices within teachers that make alternative perspectives possible also make orchestration and integration necessary for successful, reflective practice. Teachers not only must argue within themselves, but within their school contexts and cultures. Two warring voices come through loudly in the teachers' journals. Sister Mary Beth illustrates this when she writes of wanting to teach the children in ways that she knows are consistent with how children learn, yet school practice, policies, her own teacher preparation, and mandatory standards make this very difficult. Teachers are caught between technical rationality (Schön, 1983) and human complexity. Writing about what they do, and documenting children's learning makes it increasingly more difficult to adhere to these standards.

If we look at the concept of growth and teacher professional development we alluded to earlier, we find that teachers develop ego maturity with understanding of themselves and the persons they teach. They gain a sense of personal efficacy in following their intuitions. This strengthens their sense of self which in turn enables them to appreciate students as separate beings with their own interests and ways of learning. They develop the ability to use their observation mind to critically evaluate their practice, and to listen to warring factions without either jumping ship or prematurely taking sides; they can ask, 'So what's happening?' and stick around to find out.

## Supporting Educational Inquiry

It is because scientific [educational] inquiry is shot through with value judgments that no scientist [teacher] can avoid some responsibility for the judgments [s]he makes. Bacause value judgments play so important a role in scientific [educational] thinking, ways and means must be discovered of making value judgments themselves the subject matter for scientific [educational] inquiry (Cantril *et al.*, 1949, p. 19).

Research challenges our realities: our assumptions, beliefs, and conceptual frameworks. Defining research (after Stenhouse, 1985) as systematic, sustained, self-critical inquiry made public, one can begin to ferret out qualities and characteristics of those who would engage successfully in such pursuits. Research necessitates focusing attention, sustaining a scientific attitude and developing and implementing methods of inquiry which are consistent with and follow from initial and evolving questions. Research is a method and process for formative evaluation and professional development and it is dependent upon professional development for both its focus and interpretations. If research stems from the hitches we encounter in practice, from 'our inadequate understanding of the conditions giving rise to a phenomenon', discovering how we make value judgments must include investigating our assumptions and expectations.

Teachers' research and teachers' professional development were and are inextricably related. There are fundamental similarities in teachers' theorizing at all levels represented in the studies drawn from here. Teachers at the early childhood and tertiary levels wrote of their underlying struggles between their consciences and their practices, their images of themselves as professionals and what they felt was expected of them. On the one hand, they wanted to appear competent, on the other they wanted to be humane. They felt torn between what they felt to be professional expectations and their feelings of what was best for the pupils they taught. Many teachers became aware of the very different world views of their pupils and themselves. In general, teacher researchers moved from reluctance to watch themselves as researchers to include themselves in the process of research and to question their practices and learning to observe in nonjudgmental ways. Teachers found themselves describing other teachers' (or pupils') motives and then slowly turned to themselves to find those same motives. In collaborative research projects teachers moved from guardedness to relative openness with their colleagues. As teachers became more involved in their research, they also entertained alternative forms of data interpretation.

There appear to be several types of support that helped to enable teachers reported on here to develop as inquirers: a trusted or critical colleague, colleagues for informal discussion of one's inquiry, a course tutor who questioned and mirrored back some of the teacher's concerns, outside reading related to critical action research, and time and encouragement for focused attention.

### On Developing Minds that Watch Themselves

'Educational research' and 'teacher researchers' are popular topics in the literature today. Psychological health and maturity, and creativity are less popular. Yet the person who observes cannot be separated from what is observed, 'the process of knowing from what is known, what is "out there" from whatever goes on in the experiencing organism' (Cantril *et al.*, 1949). As a noted scholar of diaries put it, 'Travelling outward and inward at the same time is less a matter of physical impossibility than a condition of mental health and moral well being' (Mallon, 1984). If we really want to improve schooling, we have to improve the support given to teachers. Teachers are by definition inquirers. They begin with curiosity and what they need is an environment which supports that curiosity so that it can be sustained long enough, and with enough self-consciousness, collaboration and rigor to be the research and evaluation that are needed. As Lortie (1975) suggests, teachers fight battles with themselves and often lose. If they are to become 'researchers' into their practice they need the confidence, latitude, and resources (not the least of which are colleagues) to conduct research. Understanding how they theorize by first supporting their efforts to do so, and then observing what they say (and write), can help in the development of the kinds of policies which support professional inquiry. Importantly, teachers can become aware of the spectacles they wear and of how to help themselves and one another to develop new lenses.

### References

ARIETI, S. (1976) *Creativity: The Magic Synthesis*, New York, Basic Books.

ASSAGIOLI, R. (1973) *The Act of Will*, New York, Viking Press.

CANTRIL, H., AMES, A., HASTORF, A. and ILLELSON, W. (1949) 'Psychology and scientific research', *Science*, **110**, 4, 11, 18 November.

COMBS, A. and SNYGG, D. (1959) *Individual Behavior: A Perceptual Approach*, New York, Harper and Row Publishers.

DARLING-HAMMOND, L., WISE, A. and PEASE, S. (1986) 'Teacher evaluation in the organizational context: A review of the literature,' in HOUSE, E. (Ed.) *New Directions in Educational Evaluation*, London, Falmer Press.

DAY, C. (1987) 'The relevance of classroom research literature to the present concerns being expressed about the observation of teachers in classrooms for appraisal purposes', paper presented at the British Educational Research Association Conference, Manchester, England.

DEWEY, J. (1916) *Democracy and Education*, New York, Macmillan.

DEWEY, J. (1938) *Experience and Education*, New York, Macmillan.

ELLIOTT, J. (1989a) 'Appraisal of performance or appraisal of persons', in SIMONS, H. and ELLIOTT, J. (Eds) *Rethinking Appraisal*, Milton Keynes, Open University Press.

ELLIOTT, J. (1989b) 'Educational theory and the professional learning of teachers: An overview', *Cambridge Journal of Education*, **19**, 1, pp. 81–102.

ELLIOTT, J. (1989c) 'Teacher evaluation and teaching as a moral science', in HOLLY, M.L. and McLOUGHLIN, C. (Eds) *Perspectives on Teacher Professional Development*, London, Falmer Press, pp. 239–58.

FERRUCCI, P. (1982) *What We May Be*, New York, St. Martins Press.

FULLER, F. (1969) 'Concerns of teachers: A developmental characterization', *American Educational Research Journal*, **6**, 2, pp. 207–26.

GATES, J. (1987) 'A theatre of contradictions: Dilemmas in the role of an LEA advisor', Master of Education Thesis, Durham, University of Durham.

GITLIN, A. (1989) 'Educative school change: Lived experiences in horizontal evaluation', *Journal of Curriculum and Supervision*, Summer, **5**, 4, pp. 322–39.

HARTLEY, L. and BROADFOOT, P. (1988) 'Assessing teacher performance', *Journal of Educational Policy*, **3**, 1, pp. 39–50.

HEATH, D. (1980) 'Toward teaching as a self-renewing calling', in HALL, G., HORD, S. and BROWN, G. (Eds) *Exploring Issues in Teacher Education: Questions for Future Research*, Austin, TX Research and Development Center for Teacher Education.

HERRICK, G. (1949) *George Ellet Coghill, Naturalist and Philosopher*, Chicago, University of Chicago Press.

HILLMAN, J. (1983) *Healing by Fiction*, Barrytown, NY, Station Hill.

HOLLY, M.L. (1989) *Writing to Grow: Keeping a Personal–Professional Journal*, Portsmouth, NH, Heinemann Educational Books.

HUNT, D. (1970) 'A conceptual level matching model for coordinating learner characteristics with educational approaches', *Interchange*, **1**, 3, pp. 68–82.

JOHNSTON, C.M. (1986) *The Creative Imperative*, Berkeley, Celestial Arts.

JUNG, C. (1968) *Man and His Symbols*, New York, Dell Publishing Co.

JUNG, C. (1964) 'The basic postulates of analytic psychology', in RUITENBECK, H.M. (Ed.) *Varieties of Personality Theory*, New York, Dutton.

KELLEY, E. (1947) *Education for What is Real*, New York, Harper and Brothers.

KELLEY, E. (1962) 'The fully functioning self', in COMBS, A. (Ed.) *Perceiving, Behaving, Becoming*, Yearbook of the Association for Supervision and Curriculum Development, Washington DC, ASCD, pp. 9–20.

KELLY, G. (1955) *The Psychology of Personal Constructs*, New York, Norton.

KUHN, T. (1962) *The Structure of Scientific Revolutions*, Chicago, University of Chicago Press.

LANGER, S. (1982) *Mind: An Essay on Human Feeling*, Vol. III, Baltimore, Johns Hopkins Press.

LORTIE, D. (1975) *Schoolteacher: A Sociological Study*, Chicago, University of Chicago Press.

LUGO, J. and HERSHEY, G. (1979) *Human Development: A Psychological, Biological, and Sociological Approach to the Life Span*, New York, Macmillan.

MALLON, T. (1984) *A Book of One's Own: People and Their Diaries*, New York, Ticknor and Fields.

MASLOW, A. (1954) *Motivation and Personality*, New York, Harper and Brothers.

MASLOW, A. (1968) *Toward a Psychology of Being*, New York, Van Nostrand Reinhold.

MAY, R. (1975) *The Courage to Create*, New York, Bantam Books.

MONTAGU, A. (1989) *Growing Young*, South Hadley, MA, Bergin & Garvey.

OJA, S. (1989) 'Teachers: Ages and stages of adult development', in HOLLY, M.L. and McLOUGHLIN, C. (Eds) *Perspectives on Teacher Professional Development*, London, Falmer Press, pp. 119–54.

OJA, S. and PINE, G. (1983) *A Two Year Study of Teacher Stages of Development in Relation to Collaborative Action Research in Schools: Final Report*, Washington DC, National Institute of Education.

ORNSTEIN, R. (1986) *The Psychology of Consciousness*, New York, Penguin Books.

ORNSTEIN, R. (1987) *Multimind*, Boston, Houghton Mifflin.

*Oxford English Dictionary* (1971) Oxford, Oxford University Press.

PETERS, R. (1965) 'Education as initiation', in ARCHAMBAULT, R. (Ed.) *Philosophical Analysis and Education*, New York, Humanities.

SCHÖN, D. (1983) *The Reflective Practitioner: How Professionals Think in Action*, New York, Basic Books.

SPRINTHALL, N. and SPRINTHALL, L.S. (1980) 'Adult development and leadership training for mainstream education', in CORRIGAN, D. and HOWEY, K. (Eds) *Concepts to Guide The Education of Experienced Teachers*, Reston, VA, Council for Exceptional Children.

STENHOUSE, L. (1975) *An Introduction to Curriculum Research and Development*, London, Heinemann Educational Books.

STENHOUSE, L. (1985) *Research as a Basis for Teaching*, in RUDDUCK, J. and HOPKINS, D. (Eds) London, Heinemann Educational Books.

STRATTON, G. (1896) 'Some preliminary experiments in vision without inversion of the retinal image', *Psychological Review*, **3**, pp. 611–17.

TOM, A. (1980) *Teaching as a Moral Craft*, New York, Longman.

VON FRANZ, M.L. (1968) 'The process of individuation', in JUNG, C. *Man and His Symbols*, New York, Dell Publishing Co., pp. 157–254.

WESTON, P. (1979) *Negotiating the Curriculum: A Study of Secondary Schooling*, Slough, NFER.

WHITEHEAD, J. (1989) 'Creating a living educational theory from questions of the kind, "How do I improve my practice?"' *Cambridge Journal of Education*, **19**, 1, pp. 41–52.

# Notes on Contributors

**Colin Biott** is Reader in Education at University of Northumbria at Newcastle. He was formerly Director in INSET at Sunderland University. He has published widely on research and evaluation, especially on the subject of teacher research.

**Robert G. Burgess** is Director of CEDAR (Centre for Educational Development, Appraisal and Research) and Professor of Sociology at the University of Warwick. His main teaching and research interests are in social research methodology, especially qualitative methods, and the sociology of education, especially the study of schools, classrooms and curricula. He has written ethnographic studies of secondary schools and is currently working on case-studies of schools and higher education. His main publications include: *Experiencing Comprehensive Education* (1983), *In the Field: An Introduction to Field Research* (1984), *Education, Schools and Schooling* (1985), *Sociology, Education and Schools* (1986) *Schools at Work* (1988, with Rosemary Deem), and *Implementing In Service Education and Training* (1993, with J. Connor, S. Gallaway, M. Morrison and M. Newton) together with fourteen edited volumes on qualitative methods and education. He has been President of the British Sociological Association and is currently a member of the ESRC Training Board.

**Eleanor Chelimsky** has been the director of the US General Accounting Office's Program Evaluation and Methodology Division which conducts studies of individual government programs for the US Congress since 1980. She came to the GAO after ten years with the MITRE Corporation where she directed the corporation's work in program evaluation, policy analysis and research management. She was a Fulbright Scholar in Paris, a past president of the Evaluation Research

Society, the recipient of the 1982 Myrdal Award for Government, GAO's Distinguished Service Award for 1985 and GAO's Meritorious Executive Award for 1987. She became an Assistant Comptroller General in the General Accounting Office in December 1988.

**Mary Louise Holly** is Professor of Teacher Development, Leadership and Curriculum Studies at Kent State University, where she teaches in the areas of professional development, curriculum theory, and the arts. She has held visiting positions at the Centre for Applied Research in Education at the University of East Anglia and the School of Education at Deakin University in Australia. Her research has centred on life history, biography and journal keeping as means of interpreting teaching and professional development. She has co-edited a special issue of *The Cambridge Journal of Education* on biography in education. Other publications include *Writing to Grow: Keeping a Personal-Professional Journal* (Heinemann) and *Perspectives on Teacher Professional Development* (Falmer).

**Mary James** is Tutor in Education at the University of Cambridge Institute of Education. From 1985 to 1990 she was Deputy Director of the Pilot Records of Achievement in Schools Evaluation [PRAISE] funded by the Department of Education and Science and the Welsh Office.

**Frederick Mulhauser** is assistant director in the Program Evaluation and Methodology Division of the US General Accounting Office (GAO). Before joining GAO in 1983, he directed research funding on school management and organization at the US National Institute of Education for a decade. He has been a teacher, principal, and evaluator in schools in Massachusetts and Washington DC, and wrote school curriculum materials for Harvard Project Social Studies. He served as special assistant to Representative John Brademas in the US House of Representatives. He has been adjunct professor at the American University in Washington and holds degrees from Harvard and Yale.

**Jennifer Nias** was Tutor in Curriculum Studies 3–13 at the Cambridge Institute of Education. She worked with experienced teachers on in-service courses, but she has also worked in pre-service education (BEd and PGCE). She has published widely in the field of education, especially on the sociology of education and primary education. She is now Rolle Professor of Education at the University of Plymouth.

**Christopher Pole** holds a joint post with CEDAR and the Sociology Department, University of Warwick where he teaches Field Studies in Social Research and Sociology of Education. In CEDAR he is currently engaged in an ESRC funded research project which examines the socialization and supervision of first-year PhD students in the Natural Sciences. In addition his principal research interests are in the use and development of qualitative research methods, strategies for assessing and reporting pupils' educational achievements and pupil transfer from school to non-school. He has previously worked as a Research Officer at the National Foundation for Educational Research and at the Institute of Manpower Studies, University of Sussex.

**Alan Sanday** is an Associate Fellow in the Centre for Educational Development, Appraisal and Research at the University of Warwick. He was formerly Chief Adviser for Coventry. After graduating at Oxford, he taught in the RAF (technical education) and in Coventry and Nottingham before becoming Science Adviser and Area Inspector in Warwickshire. As well as serving on the steering committees of several national projects, he was for some time chairman of the Schools Broadcasting Council Secondary Committee. He is known chiefly for his pioneering work with Peter Birch on the 'Understanding Industrial Society' project; it has been republished as *Understanding British Industrial Society* (Edward Arnold) and is the basis of a Mode 1 Syllabus with three of the GCSE Boards. His current work involves reviewing and reanalyzing the research on School Effectiveness and School Improvement Programmes in order to make it more accessible to teachers and advisers. This is now published as CEDAR Occasional Paper No. 2 *Making Schools More Effective*.

**Brian Wilcox** was Chief Adviser of the City of Sheffield Education Department. From 1989 to October 1990 he was seconded as Director of the Training Agency-funded Inspection Methodologies for Education and Training (IMET) project. He is currently co-directing the ESRC funded Programmes to Assess the Quality of Schools (PAQS) project in the Division of Education, University of Sheffield where he is Professorial Research Fellow. His main research interest is the theory and practice of evaluation in education, training and the public services.

# Name Index

# Subject Index